SPEED
READING

SPEED READING

Robert L. Zorn, Ph.D.

PERENNIAL LIBRARY

Harper & Row, Publishers
New York, Cambridge, Philadelphia, San Francisco
London, Mexico City, São Paulo, Singapore, Sydney

To my wife, Joan

FIRST EDITION

Designer: *Janice Stern*

Library of Congress Cataloging in Publication Data
Zorn, Robert L
  Speed reading.
  1. Rapid reading. I. Title.
LB1050.54.Z67   1980   428'.4'3   79–2744
ISBN 0–06–463502–3

85 86   10 9 8 7 6 5

CONTENTS

1

How Do You Compare?

So you want to learn to speed read! Speed reading is not difficult. It's actually easy. Anyone can improve his or her reading abilities. To do so simply takes motivation and some time and practice. The secret is knowing how and what to practice. That is what this book is all about. It presents the basic steps to faster and better reading. These procedures have worked each year for thousands of people who easily doubled or tripled their reading speed in classes I taught at various schools, colleges, and universities. The methods presented here are the very same successful techniques that have worked for many people for many years.

One of the first questions most people have when becoming involved in the art of speed reading is: *"How does my present reading speed compare to that of others?"*

To answer this question, you need to know two things at the outset: your reading speed and your comprehension. Since these are the two major facets of the entire reading process, determining your normal reading rate and your average comprehension is an ideal starting point on the road to better, more enjoyable reading. You can use this information as a basis for comparison and, more important, a basis for improvement.

In order to ascertain your reading rate and comprehension, simply read the following paragraph and time how long it takes you to read the entire paragraph. It is important that you read this in a comfortable manner which reflects your average or normal rate. Do not try to go excessively fast or slow. A stopwatch would be ideal to time your reading, but any clock or watch that enables you to keep track of the seconds will do fine. Just record *in seconds* how long it takes you to read this one paragraph.

All set? Begin.

READING #1
OUR UNTAPPED READING POTENTIAL

Very few people make full use of the abilities they have as far as reading is concerned. Figures from research indicate that we use only fifteen percent of our available mental resources when we are engaged in recognizing symbols, recalling their meanings, and then assembling those meanings into some resemblance of what the writer had in mind. We would take our car to the nearest garage at once if it were working on only two of its eight cylinders. Yet we don't give our reading abilities the same consideration. Once our reading skill is properly developed, it needs only consistent and proper use to keep it in the very best condition.

How many seconds did it take you? Record your time for this first reading on the Progress Chart in the back of the book (page 143), beside Reading #1, under the heading "SECONDS." This chart will enable you to keep an accurate record of your progress.

Now then, we'll see how well you understood what you read in Reading #1 when you answer the questions in the following comprehension quiz. Don't refer back to the paragraph. If you don't know the answer or can't remember, just take a guess. There's no penalty for guessing on these questions. Remember, the idea here is simply to find some basic indication of your comprehension skills.

Place your answers on the line provided after each statement. Use the following symbols for your answers: True (T), False (F), or Not Mentioned (N). The tricky part here is the (N) for Not Mentioned. It forces the reader to remember if the topic or point in question was specifically mentioned in the paragraph. It also reduces the guessing factor that would occur in a true-false quiz where the student has a fifty-fifty chance of guessing the right answer. The insertion of *"Not Mentioned"* thus enables you to have a more accurate idea of what your comprehension level really is. Let's try this comprehension quiz.

1. Few people make full use of their ability when they read. __T__

2. The task of recognizing symbols and recalling meanings takes much energy. __F__

3. We spend more money on our cars than we spend on our reading skills. __NM__

4. We should take better care of our reading skills. __T__

5. Reading skill, like a car, needs to be overhauled at regular intervals. __T__

Now let's analyze the results of your reading efforts so we can gain a quick profile, or overview, of your reading skills in both speed and comprehension. First, we convert the seconds it took you to read that paragraph into words per minute (WPM) by using the following chart. This process will give us your actual reading rate, or speed.

Time/Sec.	10	12	15	20	25	30	35	40	45	50	60
WPM	780	590	472	354	283	236	202	177	157	141	118

If the number of seconds it took you to read the paragraph isn't shown on the chart above, divide into 7080 the number of seconds it did take you to read the paragraph. This will give us your exact WPM. Next, place your WPM score for Reading #1 in the column headed "WPM" on the Progress Chart on page 143.

To find your comprehension score, refer to "Answers to Reading Exercises," beginning on page 145.

Give yourself 20 points for each right answer on this comprehension quiz and record your score for Reading #1 in the "COMPREHENSION" column on the Progress Chart (page 143).

Your score is a percentage of accuracy which indicates your comprehension level. You have now completed the following: you read the first exercise and timed how long it took in seconds; you found your WPM; you took a quiz and discovered your comprehension level. The steps you've just completed are the hardest ones outlined in this book. From here on, everything gets easier and easier.

The next thing to do is to compare the results of your speed and comprehension scores on this first reading to those achieved on the same material by people of similar educational levels (see chart on page 5). The average adult usually reads this same paragraph at the rate of approximately 200 WPM. The average high-school student reads it at the rate of about 250 WPM, the average college student at about 325 WPM. A student in graduate school would read it at about 400 WPM.

One statistic shown on the chart opposite may surprise you: the average reading rate for adults.

WPM

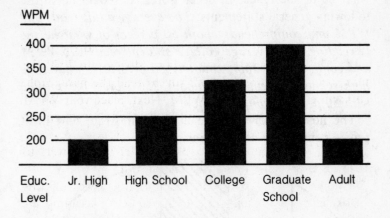

The reason most adults read at 200 WPM, even if they are college graduates, is quite simple: the amount of reading they do (once they leave school) is not anywhere near the volume they read when they were students. Therefore, their reading speed has gradually tapered off and leveled out to a rate of 200 WPM.

It is also important to note at this point that an individual's reading speed does vary somewhat, about 25 WPM plus or minus the base reading rate shown on the chart. So you can add or subtract 25 WPM from your score and then see what it does to your reading rate in comparison with the norm shown on the chart.

Keep these figures in mind as you set a goal for yourself. How fast do you wish to read? You should be able to *double* or *triple* your reading rate, at the same time maintaining or improving your comprehension.

We're now ready to examine the second major facet of reading—comprehension. It should be noted that the average person usually comprehends only about 50 percent of what he or she reads. In other words, we could make the following general statements: *The average adult reads 200 WPM and comprehends about 50 percent of what he/she is reading. The average college student reads 325 WPM and comprehends approximately 50 percent. The average high-school student reads about 250 words per minute with 50 percent comprehension.*

The normal curve can be used to illustrate how most people compare in comprehension:

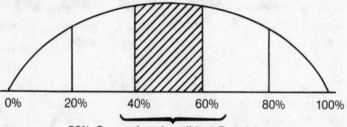

50% Comprehension (Most People)

By now you should have a good understanding of your reading abilities in both speed and comprehension. You should also have a good idea of how you compare to others. You can significantly improve both of these skills if you want to. You can become whatever kind of reader you want to be. It is not uncommon to see high-school pupils, college students, and adults increase their reading rate by 50 or 100 percent in a relatively short time, while at the same time maintaining or even increasing their comprehension!

It is important to point out that there are many myths and false conceptions about speed reading such as *Fast readers are inaccurate readers* or *Slow readers make up for their plodding along by getting more out of their reading* or *Fast readers miss everything* or *Slow readers can't be expected to improve since they weren't taught to read quickly.* All of these statements are false. This book contains proven steps which will show you how to succeed in achieving new reading skills.

Now you might say, "O.K. I can improve. You've convinced me. But how long will it take and what am I supposed to do?" The simple test of your reading speed and comprehension that you just completed already gives you some insight into the answer. Part of the answer also hinges on: *How much do you want to improve?* At what level or rate will you be satisfied with your reading?

To be more specific, some improvement will be seen in minutes! You've already taken the most important step just by reading this chapter. This book has already started you on a program to replace old reading habits with new, faster, and better reading techniques. If you are willing to practice a little as you read each day, you will be amazed at the improvement and change in your reading skills.

What about permanent improvement? If you inculcate these steps into your everyday reading habits, you will trade in your old reading skills for new ones and overhaul your reading style—permanently! There's no need for continued periodic practice or an annual retest. Speed reading is like using a muscle, to keep it in shape all you have to do is use it. As long as you use your new reading skills, you'll never revert to the old style of slow, cumbersome reading.

2

You're on Your Way!

Let's quickly review a few facts here. You know your reading speed and have a good idea of your comprehension level. You know how you compare to others who have a similar educational background. You have set a goal in terms of how fast you want to speed read. You have demonstrated the desire to improve. Now let's see if we can put it all together and watch your reading skills increase. The first step is to select a method.

THEORIES ON SPEED READING

There are many theories about how to improve one's reading rate and comprehension. The technique that has proven the most successful for most people is to change the eye movements they make in reading. In other words, the basic method of improvement is to make the eye motions or patterns more efficient. Since reading is characterized by eye movements, the question then becomes, how is this best done? This book shows you step-by-step methods to improve your eye movements over the thousands of words you read every day.

The book does not delve into other theories on reading,

such as the use of motivation or vocabulary techniques, because these methods in most instances have not achieved the desired results. For instance, there is a theory based on the rationale that a person will read faster if he or she is more interested in the material. I have found over many years of teaching reading that this is not always true. People often read slower when they like what they are reading, because they tend to savor each word or each line or each paragraph. On the other hand, some people do read faster when they read material they're deeply interested in. They become engrossed in what they're reading and the words begin to fly by. However, since some people read slower and some read faster when reading interesting material, this obviously isn't the best basis on which to improve your reading rate. It's too unpredictable and varies too much from person to person and from topic to topic.

Then there's the vocabulary method. This is based on the belief that when people build or expand their vocabulary then and only then will they read faster. But how could that be, when most people know most of the words they read every day and yet that doesn't make them read any faster. Once you're an adult, you know most of the words you see in ordinary reading matter. Even students in high school and college know *most* of the words they see every day. The fact that we periodically encounter new words does not negate our whole approach to reading speed and comprehension. (We will discuss vocabulary in more detail later in chapter 7.)

Another popular theory is that the eye will follow a moving object and therefore all you need to do is to move an object such as your finger, a pencil, or a ruler up and down the page at a fast clip and your eyes will follow accordingly so that you will soon be speed reading.

It is true that an eye will follow an object that moves across its path of vision, but who wants to depend on moving a finger or a pencil up and down the page in order to read faster? Those who like this method argue that you use these devices only in the beginning. Once you learn to read faster, you don't need them to keep your eyes moving rapidly across the printed page. But this isn't always the case because sometimes these techniques do become habit-forming.

Why not sidestep that whole debate and use a much easier method. What you want is to improve your reading so that you have the flexibility to read fast when you want to and to understand what you are reading. You wish to achieve this goal without taking a course in vocabulary building or being forced to read certain kinds of simple material so that you will read faster simply because it is easy. You don't want to rely on moving your fingers up and down a page in order to read faster.

This isn't to say these theories are all wrong. I'm simply pointing out that years of experience in teaching people of all age levels, and of varied backgrounds and education, have taught me what methods work for most people and what methods are the easiest to master. These concepts are presented for you in this book, along with practical exercises, so that you can immediately apply the new concepts of speed reading and actually see your progress.

Putting all these other theories aside, let us now look at the first secret to faster reading—improving your eye patterns. Good and bad eye movements are the result of our everyday reading habits. Very few schools teach eye patterns or movements. These movements are just assumed to evolve or happen naturally as a person learns to read.

Thus, bad habits are easily developed, which if not corrected, make us read slowly and ineffectively.

REGRESSIONS

One of the easiest habits to develop that really slows down the reader is called the *regression.* This is simply the backward eye movement or reading a word over again. Regressions are the back-up or reverse motions of the eyes. Most regressions are unnecessary and inefficient. They actually intrude on the logical sequence of the material you are reading. Some reading experts claim that *regressing is the most wasteful step in the average person's everyday reading activities.* This is just the opposite of what is often believed about reading, for many people have told me they had thought regressions improved their comprehension and speed—until they took my course. Then they found that as soon as they eliminated most of their regressions, their speed and comprehension began to increase.

Good readers glance back occasionally, but their regressions are few and far between. Let me put it this way: If you're after speed, you're not going to get it by going backward. Speed readers go forward at rapid rates with few backward eye movements.

There are two types of regressions. The *involuntary regression* is a habit from earlier years of reading. The *voluntary regression* is made under the controlled awareness of the reader to clarify a crucial point in the reading selection. The latter type of regression is occasionally needed, but should be used very sparingly.

Here is an example designed to show how both reading speed and comprehension are hindered by regressions:

Look at this sentence: NOW READ THIS QUICKLY. It contains words every adult knows. If a reader were to regress just one time on this sentence, here is how it would be perceived by the mind:

NOW READ NOW THIS QUICKLY.

Notice how awkward it is to read this sentence in its last form. What has happened is the insertion of "NOW" between the words "READ" and "THIS" because of the regression that was made. This insertion into the sequential pattern of words being sent to the brain's interpretation center is unnatural and confusing. Here is the actual pattern of the eye movements used when regressing on the word "NOW."

NOW READ THIS QUICKLY.

As you can see, a regression such as this causes confusion and certainly reduces comprehension—not to mention what it does to one's reading speed. That is why many people double or triple their reading rate and comprehension as soon as they begin to reduce or eliminate regressions. Here's how a fast reader would move his or her eyes over that same sentence:

NOW READ THIS QUICKLY.

No hesitations. No backward eye movements. No reading the same word twice. No sporadic insertion of words into the basic sentence structure.

You can eliminate or greatly reduce the number of regressions by just having an awareness or desire to reduce the regression habit. Reading once learned is a skill we put on instant replay whenever we need it. Regressions—going back over and over the letters and words as we stumble along in kindergarten or first grade—are necessary when we are first learning to read. But after that, regressions should be controlled and *not* made at random or from habit. They should be made sparingly and purposefully—in other words only when absolutely necessary.

If you don't want to rely on awareness or on trusting the eyes to self-correct this habit, there are some steps that will help you eliminate regressions. For instance, you can use a 3 × 5 index card with a *reading window* cut out of it. You make a reading-window card by measuring a rectangle 2½-inches long by ¼-inch high on a file card, then cut out the rectangle. A sample reading-window card looks like this:

READING-WINDOW CARD

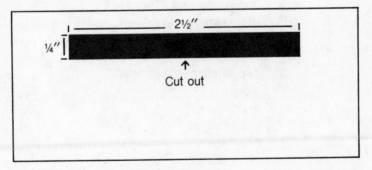

After you've made the card, place it over the following columns. Move the card down the columns. Do you see how it prevents you from regressing? Do not permit yourself to move the card up or backward at any time. Continue to move the card down until you have read the entire column. Several tries may be necessary until you get the hang of this technique.

> The lobster fisherman
> usually leaves home
> around two or three o'clock
> in the morning.
> Several miles from shore
> he reaches a number
> of large floating corks.
> Each cork is tied
> by a rope
> to a lobster trap
> on the bottom
> of the ocean.
> The traps are raised
> one by one,
> and the crawling lobsters
> are dumped
> into the covered box
> in the boat.
> The fisherman then places
> more bait
> in the traps
> and lets them
> down again.
> He often catches
> more than 100 lobsters
> in a single day.

Answer the following questions about this column. Simply underline the correct answer.

1. Fishermen, in order to catch lobsters, use: (a) nets, (b) rods and reels, (c) boxlike traps, or (d) corks.
2. The lobster fisherman's daily catch often exceeds: (a) 1000, (b) 500, (c) 5000 or (d) 100.

Now go back and find the answers in the column you've just read. How well did you read without regressions? Try it several times. You'll soon see how easy it becomes. Apply this type of drill or activity to other reading selections of your own choosing by using the reading-window card with a book or magazine you're reading. Just move it along the line of print as you read. Soon you will learn that, contrary to what many people believe, regressing does not guarantee better comprehension.

Perhaps a more detailed example of what effects regressions have on reading speed would be in order, just to emphasize this important point. Every regression a reader makes, whether voluntary or involuntary, actually slows him down because every regression takes approximately 50 WPM out of his rate of speed. If a reader, for instance, read for two hours and had only one regression per minute, just look at what would happen:

$$\begin{array}{r} 120 \text{ minutes of reading} \\ \times\ 1 \text{ regression per minute} \\ \hline 120 \text{ regressions} \end{array}$$

120 regressions $\times$ 50 WPM = 6000 words
(50 WPM is what it costs the reader for each regression)

Then, 6000 divided by 200 WPM (the rate of the average reader) equals 30 minutes spent regressing!

Therefore, this reader spent two hours reading, but a half hour of this time was spent going backwards! By now it should be obvious that you cannot read fast if regressions play a large part in your reading style.

Thus, the first step to speed reading is to become aware of and eliminate this unnecessary eye movement called regression. For the next day or two, try reading without backing up and reading words over again. See what a difference it will make. Remember that regressions for the most part are a carry-over habit from the days when we first learned how to read. One point that I cannot overemphasize is that speed readers seldom regress. This is not to say they eliminate regressions absolutely, but rather they control these backward movements so that they are few and far between. In essence, regressions do three things to the reader: (1) slow down the reading rate, (2) cause eye fatigue, and (3) hinder comprehension.

Now let's start to put theory into practice. Read the following two paragraphs, and remember: No regressions! Use the same procedure you used in the first chapter: record your time in seconds for Reading #2 on the Progress Chart in the back of the book. Watch how much improvement you will see compared to the first reading. You should be reading much faster already. Read each paragraph straight through. Give your reading a little boost of speed too!

READING #2
INSIGHT INTO REGRESSIONS

Some of the eye movements utilized in reading are actually unnecessary. One such type of movement is called a regression. This occurs when the eyes return along the line of type being read to look again at a word or words which were already seen. This movement might be considered wasteful and time-consuming and without apparent value. However, some regressions are evident even in the best readers, so they should not be viewed as totally undesirable. It is obvious to anyone who gives it much thought, however, that if it were possible to cut down on useless eye movements, reading speed and comprehension would both be improved.

Mark the following statements either True (T), False (F), or Not Mentioned (N). Place your answers on the line after each statement.

1. Most eye movements made in reading are not necessary.
   _F_

2. Regressions occur when the reader's vocabulary is inadequate.
   _F X_

3. Poor readers are likely to regress more often than good readers. _N ✓_

4. Reading would be improved by cutting down on useless eye movement. _T ✓_

5. Regressions might be considered as wasteful and without apparent value. _F X_

Time/Sec.	10	12	15	20	25	30	35	40	45
WPM	690	575	460	345	276	230	197	172	153

If your time isn't shown above, divide 6900 by the number of seconds it took you to read the paragraph. This will give you your exact WPM. (For answers, see page 145.) Now place your WPM and comprehension scores on the Progress Chart page. Now let's try another paragraph. Remember: *No regressions!*

READING #3
MORE ABOUT REGRESSIONS

The need for occasional regressions in reading is a matter of a great deal of controversy. Some say one must not regress under any circumstances, while others say that a regression for the purpose of clarifying the meaning of a particular statement is not only acceptable, but may be essential if a high degree of comprehension is to be attained. There appears to be evidence to show that even very good readers regress now and then. Inadequate recognition or a poor vocabulary may cause some regressions. The kind of material read may in some instances also influence regressions. However, there can be no doubt about the bottom line on this controversy—speed readers very seldom regress.

Now mark the following statements either True (T), False (F), or Not Mentioned (N) in the space provided.

1. It is agreed that regressions are permissible at times. __T__ x
2. The length of the line of type has an effect on regression. __N__ ✓
3. Vocabulary and recognition can be factors causing regression. __T__ ✓
4. There appears to be evidence that good readers do not regress. __F__ ✓
5. Whether or not you regress may depend on what you are reading. __N__ x

Time/Sec.	10	12	15	20	25	30	35	40	45
WPM	732	610	488	366	292	244	209	183	162

If your time isn't shown, divide 7320 by the number of seconds it took you to read the paragraph. Be sure to record your progress in the back. (For answers, see page 145.)

3

Eye Span and Thought Units

Now you're ready for the next step. The terms *phrase reading, eye span,* and *thought units* are often used to mean the same thing: how many words the reader perceives or reads at a single glance. That is, the fundamental eye movement made by every reader. Many people think that the eyes move in continuous motion over each line of print. They don't. They move in jumps and hops in a series of segments over each line. Think of a process like a movie film, which is actually a series of single frames or pictures shown at a high rate of speed so that the viewer sees the pictures in continuous motion. Reading is a similar process: viewing a series of words or letters so rapidly that we think our eyes are in continuous motion.

The secret to reading faster then becomes: *The more words you see at one time the faster you read.* Still doubt it? Try this. Ask a friend to read while you watch his or her eyes move. See if they are in continous motion or if you observe the eyes moving in jumps and jerks as they cover each line of print. If your friend is a slow reader, it will be harder to see the jumps because the eye span is so small, whereas a fast reader really clips off the words, so that you can easily see the large, sweeping eye movements.

EYE SPAN

For many people the basis of fantastic improvement in their reading speed and comprehension is simply this—a good eye span. Obviously, if you read one word at a time and then increase this eye span to two or three words at a time, your reading speed will be improved two or three hundred percent! This increase can be extended to four or five words or more—wherever your motivation and energies take you. Comprehension is also improved by this same process because words and their meanings always have more significance when they are read in association with other words. It's like a puzzle. One small piece doesn't give much suggestion of a picture. Several connected pieces give a much better indication of what the completed puzzle will look like. So it is with reading: The wider the eye span, the faster the reading speed and the bigger the comprehension picture.

With this understanding of one of the most basic eye movements made in reading, many people have embarked on various methods to improve their eye span or recognition rate. There are various methods and practice techniques that can be utilized to develop a good eye span. You should keep in mind that everyone has a basic rhythm of eye span movements. These differ or vary from reader to reader. Eye span is one of the key factors in accounting for the difference in people's reading speeds. As you will see by the following examples, there is a significant difference between the eye span of the word-by-word reader and that of the "super tough" speed reader.

Note that the word-by-word reader reads only one word at a time, while the speed reader sees almost a whole line—or at least half a line—at a time. Each reader in these examples reads from one mark (/) to the next. Read these examples and move your eyes from one mark (/) to the next and you will be able to see the difference eye span makes in reading rates:

WORD-BY-WORD READER

There/is/no/telling/how/many/different/local/
times/there/were/in/the/United/States/prior/to/the/adoption/
of/Standard/Time./

A LITTLE FASTER READER

Reports that/a monstrous/white shark/25 to/30 feet/
long/is ranging/off Montauk,/New York/on the eastern
tip/of Long Island/have divided people/into two camps:/
those who/believe the stories/and those/who don't./

FASTER YET

San Diego is/the oldest city/in California./It is
situated/on San Diego Bay./The city is/110 miles/
southeast of Los Angeles/and only 15 miles/from the
Mexican Border./It owes/it's importance/to its superb
harbor./

SPEED READER

Just exactly what is a bird?/Perhaps you could say/
a bird is an animal that flies./But butterflies fly and they
are insects,/and bats, which are mammals, also fly./
Birds, however, have feathers./No other animal has feathers./
Feathers then, and not flying,/make a bird different
from other animals./

Note that the faster the reader is, the more words he or she sees at one time. The eye span is greater as the reader reads faster. To become a faster reader you need to train yourself to see at least two to three or four words in a single eye span. This is why many people refer to this eye-span movement as phrase reading. In speed reading, you are really reading in phrases or large groups of words. You learn to do this by increasing your eye span from one word to two words to four words to five words to a whole line at one time.

There are several facts which we should go over and re-emphasize at this time. First: You read faster and comprehend more by using the eye span method. Both your speed and comprehension improve as the eye span becomes wider. The next point is that the eye span method allows you to improve your reading skills while not having to omit or skip any words. This offsets the worry many people have about losing comprehension. They want to learn to speed read but at the same time they don't want to skip any words because they're afraid of missing something. The eye span method is their answer. Comprehension doesn't suffer; speed improves; and there is no risk of missing any key words which may be critical to understanding or comprehension.

Now try the following eye span stretching exercises. The object is to train your eyes to use the eye span method to understand larger groups of words at a single glance and to develop *rhythmic* eye movements which enable you to read quickly and comfortably. This exercise is simply a series of left-to-right eye movements with your eyes reading each phrase. Push yourself and read these as fast as you can while still understanding what you are reading. It won't work unless you go faster than normal. You have to push your reading rate. Hurry!

The national sport
of the United States
is baseball.
For more
than a century,
young and old alike,
have enjoyed playing
or watching the game.
From early spring
until late fall,
players and fans
thrill to the
umpire's heady cry of
"Play ball!"
From the
rude sandlots to
well-maintained
big league diamonds,
baseball is played
in all the states.
Every year, more than
36 million spectators
attend games
played by
professional teams.
In addition
more than
50 million
watch games
played by
organized teams of
semiprofessionals and amateurs.
Radio and TV
carry play-by-play

accounts of games.
Newspapers report
results and records
in great detail.
    In and out
of season
baseball fans
everywhere
discuss the
relative merits
of teams and players.

How was that? Easy! Right? See how reading in groups of even two or three words can really improve your speed and comprehension!

Apply these techniques to the following two paragraphs, using the same procedure. Note your time and comprehension on the Progress Chart in the back so that you can watch your improvement continue to increase. Time yourself in seconds to see how long it takes to read each paragraph. Remember: NO REGRESSIONS AND TAKE BIGGER EYE–SPAN MOVEMENTS!

READING #4
EYE-SPAN READING

There are probably as many ways of speed reading as there are ways of getting dressed in the morning. However, even in getting dressed, it is necessary to put on certain things first. For example, it is impractical to put on your socks after your shoes. Along the same vein, in speed reading some basic steps must be done first. You must learn to see one or two words at a time before you can accurately see four or five. It is a case of learning to see shorter word groups before trying longer ones. Likewise, phrases are used before attempting sentences. Eye span is one of the keys to speed reading.

Mark the following statements either True (T), False (F), or Not Mentioned (N), placing your answers in the space provided.

1. There are only one or two ways to speed read. __F__
2. Some basic, specific steps must be followed. __T__
3. Long words and sentences may be successfully read by the reader at the very beginning. __T__
4. To avoid fatigue, reading should be done in a very specific manner. __T__
5. Read at one glance from the very beginning. __F__

Time/Sec.	10	12	15	20	25	30	35	40	45
WPM	708	590	472	354	283	236	202	177	157

If your time in seconds isn't above, then divide 7080 by the number of seconds it actually took you and that will give you your exact WPM. (For answers, see page 145.)

Now try the next paragraph and record your scores on the Progress Chart on page 143.

READING #5
DIGGING FOR GOLD

The search for that rich mineral called gold started men digging deep down in the ground. Perhaps the oldest gold mine in the world is a place in Africa where early miners dug for pieces of gold. Not so long ago, when modern man explored this ancient mine, the bones of one of the old miners were found deep in the ground.

Centuries ago that miner had crawled in there to seek out some gold. The ceiling of the mine had caved in and he had died there. Beside the bones of this miner of long ago were some pieces of gold he had dug out of the rock walls. And lying there, too, was the pick he had made from a deer horn.

Mark the following statements either True (T), False (F), or Not Mentioned (N).

1. The oldest gold mine in the world is in Africa. ___T___
2. Diamonds are more valuable than gold. ___N___
3. The miner's pick was made from an early type of iron. ___Y___
4. Early Cro-Magnon man dug for gold. ___N___
5. The cave fell in and trapped the miner inside. ___T___

Time/Sec.	10	12	15	20	25	30	35	40	45	50
WPM	780	650	520	390	312	260	222	195	173	156

If your time in seconds isn't shown, divide your time into 7800 and the result will give you the exact WPM. (See page 145 for answers.)

Apply this eye-span technique periodically to your everyday reading. I've found that many magazines (e.g., *Reader's Digest* and *Sports Illustrated)* are very good for practicing these speed reading methods. In fact, most magazines and periodicals are good for this purpose because they have only five to eight words per line, and narrow columns are more conducive to the eye-span type of reading. Researchers have found that this is a major reason why magazines are so popular. They not only contain interesting topics, but because of the narrow-column format, they are very easy to read. Magazines have two, three, or four narrow columns per page, while most books have just one column across the entire page. Books, such as some histories, that have very wide columns, are especially difficult to read because they require such a wide eye-span movement to get across the page. The same reasoning applies to newspapers: The front page is easier to read because the columns are narrow; the editorial section is harder because the columns are much wider. The vocabulary level of the two pages isn't much different, if at all. Magazines and paperback books with small columns and a significant amount of white space (the area between lines and words) are easy to read and conducive to practicing speed reading.

THOUGHT UNITS

The thought-unit approach is very much like the eye-span method but with a twist. The idea here is to acquire the habit of *reading one thought after another, regardless of the number of words involved.* This requires a lot of flexibility on the part of the reader because he has to really vary his eye movements in order to accommodate the various lengths of the different thoughts. This technique stresses that all concentration should be devoted to grasping the author's thoughts and ideas. The expansion of the eye span from one word to two words, and so on, is underplayed in favor of concentrating on the large blocks of thoughts presented in the writing.

For instance, here is how a paragraph may be read by the thought-unit approach:

Today is March 21st./It is a beautiful day./It is
also my birthday./I wonder/who'll remember that?/

The exact unit of thought is subject to the reader's interpretation of what constitutes that basic thought. The only drawback to the thought-unit method is that it often requires more flexibility than the average reader possesses. Remember, most readers read one word at a time, and they read one word after another in horizontal sequence across each line. To expect them to shift to a varying eye pattern that is never the same is a lot to ask. However, it is an excellent technique if you can master it because it offers a greater potential for speed, or WPM.

Regardless of whether you like the eye-span method or the thought-unit approach, reading experts agree that one of the basic secrets of speed reading is taking in large, meaningful groups of words at one glance. The person who looks at each word or perhaps at only two words at a glance is able to pick up only small scraps of ideas. Such a practice retards his speed and impairs his comprehension. Therefore it is important to cultivate the habit of taking in as large an "eyefull" of words as you can at each glance. Proponents of the thought-unit theory say you shouldn't just take in any group of words—you should take in groups of ideas.

You should practice forcing yourself to read as fast as you can. If you consciously strive to read faster for a while, new speed patterns will replace the old ones and rapid reading will become a permanent habit. The following paragraph shows you how to grasp meaningful word groups or thought units. See if you can take in an entire group of words at each glance. Push your mental tempo as fast as you possibly can and still get the idea expressed in each word group. Try it on this example:

JOGGERS

Only a few years ago/if you thought about runners at all,/you thought of those few young men/who ran gasping around the track/at the local stadium./My, how things have changed./Today's *joggers* are everywhere./Even the term "jogger"/has found new meaning/and become a household word./Today it is not uncommon/to see men and women of all ages/jogging everywhere from around the backyard/to around the neighborhood./

Now divide the remainder of the selection that follows into thought groups as you see them. There's no right or wrong way. Just make a short mark between the word groups as was done in the preceding paragraph. After you have divided the paragraph into thought units, see if you can re-read the paragraph quickly, taking in each thought unit with one swift eye glance. This new skill takes time and practice to learn, but applying it to everyday reading will soon pay off for you!

The lean long-legged runners/of today's newest craze/ are enthusiasts of the first order./They run in summer, winter, fall, or spring./They even run in the rain/or in ten or twelve inches of snow./They run on the road/ They run along the road/ Today's runners/can be seen running everywhere./ So by now you've come to accept/the dozens of people running/through the neighborhood,/ but have you ever given it/any thought yourself?/Have you ever said to yourself./ *I must be missing something terrific?*/ Have you ever/ said to yourself *I wonder why/those people run/when they look/as if they're in pain?*/Well, the scientific fact is that/jogging is a way of running to better health./There are solid physiological/and medical reasons why jogging is good for you/Try it./

CONCLUSION

Basically, the two approaches (eye-span and thought-unit) are saying the same thing to the person who is learning to speed read. That is, increased reading speed and comprehension are dependent upon reading in larger and larger word groups. Whichever technique you use—eye-span or thought-unit—is really up to you. It is important for you to try both methods and then stick with the one that gives you the best results and feels most comfortable.

In the final analysis, everyone can learn to read in larger word groups with a reasonable amount of practice. You just have to practice and keep at it until you have it mastered. Your reward will be a reading speed that is much faster than you ever thought possible, and you'll find that your comprehension has also improved.

But don't be overly concerned about your comprehension at this early stage of the game. Concentrate on each step as it is presented. Study all the new techniques until you've mastered them. Then you can concentrate on the content. First you eliminate regressions, then you increase the eye span. Comprehension will follow. It may surprise you, but there's a lot of similarity in learning to type and learning to speed read. They both involve eye movements. A good typing teacher will tell you that at first you have to sacrifice accuracy and start to practice typing faster. Once your typing speed is where you want it, then you work at accuracy. So it is in reading with speed and comprehension; but we'll delve into this in more detail in chapter 7. Right now just concentrate on following these techniques as they are presented and getting your reading speed going.

Before we leave this chapter, let us address ourselves to one last argument occasionally heard in the field of speed reading. This is the theory that reading is not primarily a physical act involving eye movements but a psychological process which takes place in the reader's mind. That argument, followed to its logical conclusion, would mean that in order to improve a reader we should send him to a psychologist. Or does it mean that to teach speed reading we should deal with the way a person thinks instead of how he or she actually reads? To me, this is like saying that people who want to lose weight should think about their mental processes instead of watching their diet and counting calories. It is usually through becoming aware of what we are eating, re-educating ourselves as to the caloric value of different foods, and consuming fewer calories that we lose weight. So it is with reading. You first become aware of your eye patterns; then you learn to speed read by eliminating unnecessary eye movements and replacing them with more efficient ones. Isn't that what a doctor tells a patient on a diet to do—replace certain foods with more efficient ones? Overweight and slow reading are the results of excessive movements; one is toward food in the refrigerator which is not needed; the other is toward eye movements which aren't needed.

In any event, it is easier to teach a person how to count calories and how to speed read than to deal with the psychology of mind processes. I'm sure you agree.

As you read from now on, remember: *No regressions!* Move right along. Push forward every time you feel the urge to regress. Don't linger on any words. Just keep moving! Don't worry about your comprehension right now. It will come along. Stretch your eye span. Keep on reading and using these techniques. Use them every day. *You're on your way to better and faster reading!*

4

Three Major Types of Readers

There are three basic types of readers. It is important to know which type of reader you are so that you can keep progressing and improving your reading.

MOTOR READERS

The first type is called a *motor reader*. The term *motor* as used here is synonymous with movement. Motor readers move some part of the body as they read. They might wiggle their ears or nose. Maybe they chew gum or twitch an eyebrow as they read along or maybe they twirl their hair. Perhaps they always tap their fingers or move their Adam's apple as they read. Or they may move their tongue or lips or swing their legs. For them, reading and body movement are synchronized into one intertwined process. Take away the body movement and you take away these people's reading comprehension, because their reading style is disrupted. For them the faster the body movement, the faster the reading speed. The slower the body movement, the slower the reading speed.

Several of my students who were motor readers come to

mind here. First, there was Joe. I was teaching an adult education class in speed reading at the local YMCA. Joe was a college student taking the course because he wanted to go into dentistry and was worried about the amount of required reading he would face in graduate school.

During the break on the first night of class, he said to me. "I've never tried to read so fast in all my life." A few minutes later, he said, "For some reason, my legs are killing me." Sure enough, whenever Joe would read, he would shimmy his legs. No wonder he was tired—twenty minutes of fast reading to him meant twenty minutes of fast leg movements. He was a motor reader. The faster he read, the faster he tried to move his legs.

Then there was Tom. He was a motor reader too. He moved his ears when he read. At slow reading speeds, he moved only his right ear. At higher rates, both ears moved. As a young high-school student with aspirations of becoming a lawyer, he would have a lot of reading to do, and he didn't want to rely on moving his ears to read better and faster.

Of course, dependency upon moving a part of the body in order to read isn't a very good idea in the first place. It kills reading flexibility and speed, for you can read no faster than you move a part of the anatomy.

Motor readers are the slowest of the three basic types of readers. To correct this habit—and that's what it is, a habit—you first have to become aware of what you're doing. Have somebody watch you read for a few minutes and tell you if you're moving your head or wiggling your nose while you read. If you are, then you will have to work on eliminating this habit as well as learning the new speed reading steps as they are presented in this book.

AUDITORY READERS

The second type is called an *auditory reader*. Auditory readers usually read faster than motor readers because they don't rely on physical movement. Auditory readers, as the name (from the Latin *audire,* to hear) implies, rely on hearing the words.

Auditory readers, even in silent reading, form the words as if they were speaking them. It is as though they are see-ing the printed symbols while at the same time hearing the sounds associated with those words. Reliance upon sound-ing words in order to read means that the reader is slowed down to the rate of oral reading: that is, he can read no faster than he can speak.

There are many variations in auditory reading:

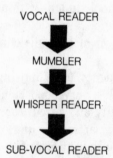

VOCAL READER

MUMBLER

WHISPER READER

SUB-VOCAL READER

Let's first look at *vocal readers,* who are the slowest group of auditory readers. Vocal readers actually say the words aloud as they read. You've probably heard these readers in the library. They think they're reading to them-selves, but everyone around them can hear them. It isn't uncommon when the librarian says *"ssssh,"* for the audi-tory readers to wonder who the librarian is referring to.

Those on the next level, the *mumblers,* aren't much better in terms of reading rates; but since mumbling is quicker than saying each word distinctly, the *mumbler reader* is a little faster than the vocal reader. Mumblers sort of read along, saying the words almost under their breath. Sometimes they sound as though they're humming their way through the printed page. It is not uncommon to see someone use this method when studying for a big exam. Relying on hearing the words as they are softly mumbled is a definite deterrent to speed and makes the reading process awkward and cumbersome. What's more, it is not essential for comprehension, which is the reason most mumblers give for continuing to use the technique.

Following this line of logic, the next fastest readers in the auditory group are the *whisper readers.* These people don't say each word aloud or even mumble along. They sort of whisper every other word or perhaps occasional words. Whisper readers use a vocal process similar to that used by mumbler readers. The only difference is in the degree of the vocalization, and that's why the whisper reader reads a little faster than the vocal or mumbler reader.

Somewhere between the whisper readers and the next group of auditory readers are the *vibrator readers.* This time the movement is made for the purpose of sounding out the words being read. Vibrator readers move the tongue or the Adam's apple as they read. Sometimes such movement cannot even be seen. Try this to see if you are a vibrator reader: Place a pencil in your mouth or chew gum while you read. Do you feel your tongue move? Or place your fingers on your Adam's apple and read. Do you feel vibration? If you answer yes to either of these questions, you unconsciously use part of your voice mechanism to sound out words as you read. Your reading is geared to that auditory process and it is holding back your reading speed. Just think how much faster you could read if you weren't waiting for those sound vibrations!

Then there are the *subvocalizers*. This is actually the trickiest form of auditory reading. There is no vocalization of words out loud, no mumbling, no whispering and no vibrations. The subvocalizer *hears each word mentally* as he reads. Thus, the term *"sub"* (meaning under) *vocalizer.*

The auditory reading process is, in my opinion, largely a result of learning to read by the phonics method of sounding out each word or letter or group of letters. It works like this:

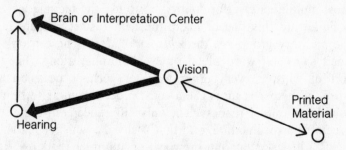

The vision picks up the printed symbols and sends an image of the symbol (letter, word, etc.) to the brain. Simultaneously, that same visual cue triggers a sound (associated with the printed symbol) and also sends that to the brain. Both signals converge in the reader's interpretation center, and this process results in auditory reading. If the auditory signal does not come through loud and clear, comprehension is about zero. Remember, the auditory reader relies on hearing the words in order to achieve comprehension. It is like the story about a neighbor of mine. His driver's license had expired and he had to take the exam over again. He passed the eye test. He passed the driving test. But he flunked the written exam. When I asked him what happened he said, "I had my new false teeth in, so I couldn't pronounce any of the words on the written test. That's why I didn't understand any of it. If I can't pronounce the words, I can't read anything."

But the strangest aspect about auditory readers is the conditions under which they enjoy reading. They like to read in either of two quite different environments.

Many auditory readers need quiet in order to read. This way, they can hear the words mentally and sound them out while they are reading. It's almost as if they are holding a conversation with themselves. They are reading, but they are also sounding out or saying each word mentally. Noisy conditions interfere with this auditory process in the reader's brain. The loud noise disrupts the reader's conversation with himself or, more precisely, the flow of sound into the brain.

Once many years ago I taught a speed reading class for senior citizens at a nearby rest home. There was a large fan in the classroom, and the group said at the outset of the first class that they couldn't read with such noise. They asked me to turn off the fan "so they could concentrate." What they wanted was to have it quiet enough to subvocalize the words they were reading. They were auditory readers. You might ask—all of 'em? Yes, all of them.

Reading, unfortunately, is sometimes taught like the style or fashion trend of skirts—what's in one year isn't necessarily in the next year. For many years teaching by phonics, or auditory reading, was in. Then teaching by the sight-reading method came back. There is much debate among reading experts about which method of teaching reading is better: phonics or sight. The pros and cons of this topic have gone on for many years. Neither side has ever gained conclusive enough proof to totally substantiate its case and thereby eliminate the opposition. And so the debate continues and the teaching of reading varies from one generation to another.

Quite often, you can tell how people read just by their age because of the reading style that was taught during the time when they were learning to read. In the case of this senior citizens group, we surveyed the group and found they had indeed all learned to read by phonics. So for that group and this kind of reader in general, quiet conditions are essential or at the very least, shall we say, greatly preferred.

The other ideal condition for an auditory-phonics reader is to read under the opposite set of circumstances, in other words, noise. Hard to believe, but some auditory readers prefer to read when there is some noise around! This is especially true for today's young auditory readers, who like to study or read with TV or music as a background. They become so engrossed in hearing themselves mentally as they read along that if someone turns off the TV, the world seems to suddenly come crashing down. The TV or radio is actually a background cover so they can concentrate on the hearing-reading process. This sound blocks out many of the little extraneous noises that would otherwise interrupt this kind of auditory reader. If it is totally quiet and then a little noise comes from somewhere else in the house, this type of reader loses concentration. Such auditory readers do better when they read in a noisy environment.

When I was going to college I can remember very distinctly seeing these two types of auditory readers. One type I would see in the student union where it was noisy. Here the students could read and mentally hear the words with all the hubbub covering any distractions. The other type of auditory reader could be seen in the library. I'd walk by and see students reading and forming the sounds of the words with their lips. In both situations the readers relied on hearing words in order to read.

SIGHT READERS

The last major type of readers are the *sight readers*. Sight reading is the instant understanding of the printed symbol without auditory association. It is the fastest form of reading because it does not involve any reliance on sound or physical movement. Thus, reading speed and comprehension are not hindered by additional steps. Sight readers see a word or group of words and instantly perceive a visual image along with the meaning associated with the printed symbol. This is why sight readers read so much faster than motor readers and auditory readers. This does not mean that sight readers always read in large word groups or have good eye spans or do not regress. It simply means that the time required for them to obtain meaning from the printed code is quicker than it is for the other two types of readers. Sight readers usually have an easier time learning to speed read because they have fewer habits to break and fewer factors slowing down their WPM.

One thing is sure: Regardless of what kind of reading a person does, he cannot rely on physical movements or auditory processes when reading fast. You may have seen demonstrations of speed reading. Well, did you ever see a speed reader waiting until his or her ears moved or vocalizing to hear how the words sounded in order to read faster? On the contrary, a speed reader zips over paragraphs and flies through the pages at a rate that seems fantastic to the novice. Such speed readers use the very same techniques you're now reading about.

CORRECTING BAD HABITS

Once you know which of the three groups of readers you belong to, how can you improve? For instance, if you're a motor reader, what can you do to increase your reading speed? First, find out which part of the body you're moving. Then you have to stop moving that part of yourself and concentrate on speed. This may not be as easy as it appears because an initial loss in comprehension usually occurs when a motor reader first stops using the motor process. This comprehension loss is soon overcome by time and practice. Then comprehension is even better, for it no longer is dependent on another process.

Did you ever see the frustrated look of someone trying to read in a noisy place? It takes a long time to read when you have to re-read the passages because you're grasping for the sounds. As you cut down on vocalizing or relying on auditory reading, your attention shifts from the sounding of words to the meaning of words. You no longer rely on the sound of every word, so you read faster. Push yourself to go faster. Get some speed! If you have to, you'll still hear enough words to get the meaning. In the meantime, you're constantly reducing your reliance on the auditory reading process. Go for the WPM! Go faster than you think you should. You've got to get moving. Stretch your abilities.

As with learning any new skill, you can best master speed reading by practice. Try speed reading the next three paragraphs with no regressions, a good swift eye span and no physical movements, no auditory processes.

Think of these paragraphs as exercises or calisthenics—you're going to push yourself to do your fastest and best time yet.

Put your scores for #'s 6, 7, and 8 on the Progress Chart on page 143. (For answers, see pages 145–146.)

READING #6
HOW OUR EYES MOVE IN READING

When we read our eyes do not move smoothly along the line of print. They jump or hop from spot to spot like a runner in a hurdle race—he runs, then jumps, then runs and then jumps again. That's the way we read. It is during the brief stops or pauses that reading actually takes place. We do not read while our eyes are in motion. If we see several words at each pause, we read more rapidly. If we see one word at a time, we read slowly. The more words we see, the faster we read. By widening the span of vision used, we improve our reading speed and comprehension.

Mark the following statements either True (T), False (F), or Not Mentioned (N).

1. Our eyes move smoothly in reading. _____
2. Fast readers see several words in one eye movement. _____
3. Slow readers forget what they read. _____
4. Movements made in running a hurdle race are similar to those made in reading. _____
5. By widening the span of vision used, we improve our reading abilities. _____

Time/Sec.	10	12	15	20	25	30	35	40	45	50
WPM	732	610	488	366	293	244	209	183	163	146

If your time in seconds isn't shown, divide the number of seconds it took you to read the paragraph into 7320 and this will give you your exact WPM. (For answers, see page 145.)

READING #7
LIVING IN A SORORITY HOUSE

One young woman, an only child, chose to live in a sorority house in order to better learn to live with others. She considered sorority-house living to be an invaluable experience. She said that someone "living in the house becomes more involved in sorority activities. People depend on you to do more, and so you do. You learn to become involved." She went on to say, "You don't have a whole lot of privacy with all those people in one house, but you learn how to get along. After a while it's like having one big family."

Mark the following statements either True (T), False (F), or Not Mentioned (N).

1. Living in a sorority teaches you how to live with others.
   _____

2. The young sorority sister was very wealthy. _____
3. Involvement is a by-product of living in a sorority house.
   _____

4. There is a lot of privacy. _____
5. The sorority house where this young woman lived was on the campus of a major midwestern state university. _____

Time/Sec.	10	12	15	20	25	30	35	40	45	50
WPM	636	530	424	318	254	212	181	159	141	127

If your time in seconds isn't shown, divide your time

(number of seconds) into 6360 and this will give your exact WPM. Don't forget to keep track of all your progress—time, comprehension, and WPM—in the back of the book on the Progress Chart (page 143). Remember, you're going for S-P-E-E-D! Push your abilities. You don't have to remember every detail. Go for SPEED! SPEED! SPEED!

READING #8
A GROWING FUTURE FOR FOREST POWER

In this age of energy shortages when the surging price of oil products is bad news for many people, there looms a new hope on the horizon—forest power. Some energy experts say forest power, otherwise known as *wood,* is rapidly becoming a realistic alternative to oil products. In the past few years as a result of the resurgence of forest power, the wood-stove industry has been brought back to life. Good old-fashioned Yankee ingenuity has once again shown its flexibility in meeting the needs of contemporary living. Fireplaces are used more than ever in recent times as people search for solutions to heating bills. Dependency on foreign oil has also alarmed some Americans enough to look to alternate fuel sources such as forest power.

Mark the following statements either True (T), False (F), or Not Mentioned (N).

1. Forest power is a new hope as an alternate fuel source.
   _____

2. The Middle East currently supplies 80 percent of all oil imported into the U.S. _____

3. Dependency on foreign oil has not alarmed some Americans.
   _____

4. Forest power is another example of Yankee ingenuity. _____
5. The wood stove and fireplace are once again enjoying a resurgence of popularity. _____

Time/Sec.	10	12	15	20	25	30	35	40	45	50
WPM	816	680	544	408	326	272	233	204	181	163

If your time isn't shown above, divide into 8160 by the number of seconds it took you to read this paragraph and that will give you your exact WPM. (For answers, see page 146.)

Look back over your calculations now on the Progress Chart; and if you have pushed yourself, there should be a significant increase in your WPM and your comprehension should be as good as (or better than) when you started. You know now how to lift your normal reading rate to a higher and higher speed. Success will not always come in a few days or even a few weeks. You are in the process of breaking lifelong habits and establishing new ones. Sometimes that takes a while. Sometimes, however, success is instant. It all depends on the individual reader. Breaking the speed barrier can be fun. Keep at it. Now let's see how to measure your reading speed on books, magazines, or articles and how you should practice to keep on developing your newfound reading abilities.

5

Measuring Your Reading Speed and How to Practice

It's important to know how and what to practice if you are going to keep on mastering the art of speed reading. Your reading ability can be improved if you: 1) want to improve, 2) know how to improve, and 3) practice. By getting this book, you've already demonstrated a desire to improve, so step one has already been accomplished. Knowing how to improve depends to a great extent on my job as author to show you the methods or techniques for improving your reading. Since you're now up to chapter 5, we're making progress on this second step. This brings us to step three: practice. This last one is really up to you and that's what this chapter is all about. Research has shown that with practice almost anyone can make at least a 20 percent improvement in reading rate.

There is no one established pattern for practice that is applicable to everyone. That's the beauty of the methods found in this book—flexibility. For instance, you can choose the old, proven, standby procedure of setting aside a time for practice each day. That's been a time-tested successful way of learning almost anything. Or you could do the opposite—have no established time for practice and just incorporate the techniques found in this book into your daily reading whenever you can. This is a gradual, periodical process. We'll explore these two different methods in more detail in just a bit, but first let's see how to measure your reading speed on material you read from a magazine, journal, nonfiction book, or your favorite novel. Then we can incorporate this procedure into our explanation of practicing by the two different methods just discussed.

MEASURING YOUR READING SPEED

First you have to remember where you begin to read. Maybe place a mark (✓) where you start. Then read as fast as you can but still read with understanding. Speed—not sheer recklessness at all costs. Reading so fast that you cannot follow the author's thoughts will accomplish nothing. Yet you have to keep in mind, too, that you still have to work at cranking up your reading speed. The whole idea of this book is to learn to speed read, and you'll learn that best by doing it. Remember, at this stage your primary objective is speed! Thus in your practice first you place a mark (✓) where you start and then when you finish reading your selection, make another mark (✓) where you finish.

In addition to keeping track of where you started and finished, you will want to ascertain your time in seconds indicating how long it took you to read the material. The length of the reading is up to you, but shorter readings of one to four paragraphs at the outset of learning to speed read will be better for our purposes.

Perhaps the time box will show how this works:

Finishing time: _____
Starting time: − _____
Reading time: _____ (seconds)

Next you find the total number of words in what you have read. This is called the word count. An easy way to do this is to count the number of words in one line of average length, then multiply that by the number of lines you have read. This way you don't have to count each word. *When counting words, remember that contractions, hyphenated words, or numbers with decimal points or commas are counted as two words.*

The third step is to multiply the word count by 60. This gives us a result that we call *total words*. Then divide the total words by the number of seconds it took you to read that material. Now you have your exact reading speed in words per minute (WPM). The whole process of finding your reading rate would be like this:

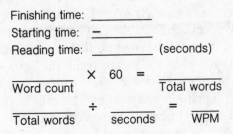

Finishing time: _____
Starting time: — _____
Reading time: _____ (seconds)

_____ × 60 = _____
Word count   Total words

_____ ÷ _____ = _____
Total words   seconds   WPM

Here's a sample calculation:

Finishing time: 1:51 P.M.
Starting time: 1:30 P.M.
Reading time: 21 (seconds)

Word count 118 × 60 = Total words 7080
Total words 7080 ÷ 21 seconds = 337 WPM

This procedure is a simple method to convert time in seconds to words per minute. You can use it daily to check on your reading speed for whatever material you choose to read. You simply need two pieces of information:

1. The number of words in the selection you have read.
2. The number of seconds it took you to read it.

Another way to look at the formula or this process is:

$$\frac{\text{number of words in selection} \times 60 = \text{(total words)}}{\text{time in seconds}} = \text{WPM}$$

Timed practice with light, easy-to-read nonfictional material is best. Technical material is difficult to use as a basis for practice when you are learning this new skill. In your approach, concentrate first on speed; comprehension and recall will follow. Probably the hardest aspect of speed reading is worrying about comprehension. Learning to read faster is like learning to swim faster or to run faster. At first, things seem awkward. It takes time and practice before the new ways feel comfortable, easy, and natural. If you want to test your comprehension on these timed practice readings, see if you can jot down or recall the author's main points. Try to remember the basic plot or major points of the story. Then hand the article, book or magazine to a friend or family member and ask him or her to quiz you about what you have just read.

Here's a sample reading for your application of the formula just explained.

READING #9
COLONIAL WILLIAMSBURG

Colonial Williamsburg is the term popularly used to refer to the restoration and preservation of eighteenth-century Williamsburg, Virginia, that was begun many years ago. The Colonial Williamsburg Foundation is the corporate name of the organization that carries on the restoration, preservation, and related educational programs.

Colonial Williamsburg has an appeal for everyone in every season. Among these appeals are the many buildings furnished with outstanding English and American antiques, the colonial crafts program, the boxwood gardens, the numerous cultural and educational activities. Most important, Williamsburg recalls to present and future generations the lasting concepts of American government and individual liberty that were developed there over two centuries ago.

Now mark the following statements either True (T), False (F), or Not Mentioned (N).

1. Colonial Williamsburg is near Boston, Massachusetts. _____
2. The corporate name of the agency in charge is the Colonial Williamsburg Foundation. _____
3. Williamsburg is only open in the summer for the ·tourist season.

_____
4. Colonial Williamsburg was originally funded by the Rockefeller Foundation. _____
5. Colonial Williamsburg is a restoration of eighteenth-century life in America. _____

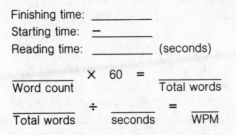

Finishing time: _____
Starting time: − _____
Reading time: _____ (seconds)

$$\frac{\rule{2cm}{0.4pt}}{\text{Word count}} \times\ 60\ =\ \frac{\rule{2cm}{0.4pt}}{\text{Total words}}$$

$$\frac{\rule{2cm}{0.4pt}}{\text{Total words}} \div\ \frac{\rule{2cm}{0.4pt}}{\text{seconds}}\ =\ \frac{\rule{2cm}{0.4pt}}{\text{WPM}}$$

The exact word count should be 114. When you time yourself and use the formula as shown, you will actually be coming up with an estimated word count. This will, however, give you a close enough approximation of your word count to enable you to quickly obtain some indication of your reading speed. The word count for that paragraph of 114 x 60 equals 6840 total words, which, divided by the number of seconds it took you to read the paragraph, equals your WPM!

PRACTICE CHANGING YOUR READING HABITS

A point of caution or advice about practicing is in order. Today we have many gadgets and machines that do a lot of work for us. These are convenient and save us time and energy, but they often lead people to believe in easy solutions. TV puts on weekly miracles that solve crimes and monumental problems in thirty minutes or less. This leads many people to believe there are ways of accomplishing goals without work or effort. That may be true for some things, but not many. In fact, I don't know of many purposes that can be fulfilled without effort or energy. The bigger the accomplishment, the bigger the expenditure of effort usually required. Speed reading falls into the category of learning that requires concentration and effort. Once mastered, however, it only takes periodic use to keep it working. It's like a muscle that needs only regular exercise to keep in shape.

To change your reading habits, first look at your present reading patterns. Like regressions, for example. Do you make many regressions? Do these help you to attain a good reading speed? Obviously they do not. *But if you intend to improve, then you should make a plan that includes* positive *ingredients.* A plan cannot be based on what you say you are *not* going to do. Instead, it should indicate what you *are* going to do. For example, if you say to yourself, "I'm not going to regress," then all you think of is regressing. A better method would be to say, "I'm going to keep going to the next phrase. I'm going to push on." It is a little like dieting. If all you think of is not eating, then eating is still on your mind. You have to replace the negative thought with a positive one. In order to eliminate a bad habit, you have to do three things. First, become aware that the habit exists. Second, have the desire to change. Third, set up and practice on the opposite of the negative habit: that is, your goal. Think about *going forward* instead of *not regressing*.

Your plan, whatever it is, must be small in terms of time and what you are going to accomplish. For example, you might set a plan of reading fast for one minute out of every fifteen. In terms of time this plan is the opposite of "I'm going to speed read everything from now on." One aim is small and definite and accomplishable. The other is grandiose and sounds good but is seldom achievable in realistic terms. The small plan allows you to see daily success and receive positive reinforcement for your efforts as you progress. It allows you to feel good about yourself as you change your reading habits. The other plan is vague and provides few opportunities to realize daily positive reinforcement.

A specific plan is what is needed. You should know exactly what steps you are working on. Plans like "I'm going to be a good reader" are worthy but too vague. Set specific goals for your reading and what you expect to accomplish. You might set your goal as simply as "I'm going to read this page as fast as I can."

Good plans that ultimately change our reading habits are *repetitive*. Plan something you can do fairly often so that it becomes part of your new regular reading habits.

All these ingredients will help you to change your reading habits. When you practice your reading, don't try to work on too many concepts at one time. Single out one method and work on that until you feel comfortable with it. Then go to the next. You might want to use a *reading do-plan*. A do-plan is based on all the concepts I've just explained. It is what you plan to do. It is based on the *positive, small, specific,* and *repetitive* aspects of changing the way you read. Here's a sample do-plan from one of the students I had in class not too long ago. Susan is a young nursing supervisor who was swamped with lots of reading in her profession. She said the do-plan method helped her achieve definite goals each day.

DO-PLAN FOR SPEED READING

Daily Do-Plan   May

Read 5 pages and force eyes to always go to the next phrase.

1	2	3	4	5	6	7	8
✓	✓	✓	✓				

As you can see, her goal is placed on the left. It is small, very specific, positive, repetitive and can be accomplished in a very short time. Each day Susan achieved that goal she felt the positiveness of speed reading and her efforts seemed more worthwhile. It is with such methods that old habits are changed and new ones are built—in reading or in just about anything else you care to accomplish.

This do-plan method is also called the short-range technique because it doesn't take long to improve this way. You set aside time for practice each day and really go at it. You have a definite plan. You usually see progress right away. Practice is concentrated and follows a definite routine. You clear away all other distractions. You make that phone call or finish that task before devoting all your energies to reading and practicing the concepts as presented in this book. You really concentrate. This do-plan style of learning to speed read is similar to the method of swimmers you see on the beach who go rushing into the water with definite, planned movements. They jump right into things and get them over with. Others like to tip the toe into the water, come back out, and gradually work their way in again. They might repeat the process over and over until they're used to the water. They're using the *periodic* method. This takes a little longer in getting into the water and also in learning to speed read. It's all a matter of individual preference. The idea is that they all get into the water, and you can all get into speed reading, but you have to work at it. Pick a method and keep at it.

Now let's put theory into practice on a few paragraphs. Remember to make a conscious effort to go for speed. No regressions, keep going forward, read in phrases or thought units and with a good eye span, don't rely on auditory methods. Remember, too, no physical movements. Trust in your new abilities and let your eyes fly over the material. Use the Progress Chart page in the back of the book to keep track of your progress.

READING # 10
SPORTS AND READING

Any good athlete will tell you he practiced long and hard to get in shape and achieve high honors. We seldom hear of any athlete becoming a champion without any effort. Do we expect to be able to run the hundred-yard dash without training? No, we consider training to be a part of the game. Once he is in shape, it is easier for an athlete to keep in condition. Reading skills develop the same way. Any person who can see words and has the desire, can learn to read faster and with understanding.

Mark the following statements either True (T), False (F), or Not Mentioned (N).

1. Good athletes practice long and hard. _____
2. Learning to speed read takes practice. _____
3. Reading skills develop naturally. _____
4. We expect to be able to run the hundred-yard dash without training. _____
5. Anyone who can see and is motivated can improve his or her reading. _____

Time/Sec.	10	12	15	20	25
WPM	606	505	404	303	242

If your time isn't shown, divide into 6060 for your exact WPM. (For answers, see page 146.)

READING #11
HOLIDAY INNS

Holiday Inns are located all across America and can be found in every major city in the nation. The Holiday Inn philosophy, according to their advertisements, is simple. It is to give you the most important things when you travel. Their ads say only Holiday Inn gives you the widest choice of the most popular locations, wherever you travel. You can choose among a variety of locations in and around town. Or take your choice of locations throughout the suburbs or all along the highways. So you can be right where you want to be.

Next, they say everything in their hotels must measure up to their "no surprise" standards. Things you notice; for example, every mattress must be comfortable—specified *Manufacturer's Top of the Line*. Right down to things you might not notice like cleaning your carpet every day. These are some of the reasons why Holiday Inns say they please more travelers than anybody else. They think they should be # 1 in pleasing you.

Mark the following statements either True (T), False (F), or Not Mentioned (N).

1. Holiday Inns are found around the world. _____
2. The Holiday Inn philosophy is simple. _____
3. The Inns must measure up to "no surprise" standards.
   _____
4. The Holiday Inns were the first popular, nationwide family hotel chain in America. _____
5. The Holiday Inns think they should be # 1 in pleasing you.
   _____

Time/Sec.	10	12	15	20	25	30
WPM	1026	855	684	513	410	342

If your time isn't shown, divide the number of seconds it took you to read the story into 10,260. That will give you your speed or WPM for the Progress Chart. (See page 146 for answers.)

6

More Techniques That Work

Another eye movement that is critical to a good reading speed is called *return eye sweep*. This is the movement that your eyes make as they go from the end of one line to the beginning of the next. It should be a very rapid movement, just as the word *sweep* implies. The eyes should have a return which is smooth, rapid, and rhythmic.

The drill on page 57 should make you conscious of correct eye movements which should be made during the return sweeps. Read the paragraph quickly. Your eyes should make two eye spans or jumps per each line of the paragraph. At the end of the line, make your eyes follow the dotted arrows which show you the return-eye-sweep pattern.

Did you feel the sweep of your eyes? Now go back and try to read this same exercise even more rapidly. Race your eyes along the arrows. Never give your eyes a chance to stop or waver as they move from the end of one line to the next. This forcefulness and direct movement is the key to improving your return sweep. If your eyes waver, they may lose the place. If your eyes linger or hesitate, your reading speed suffers. If your eyes move quickly and smoothly on the return sweep, they will reach their destination accurately and your reading rate will be much faster.

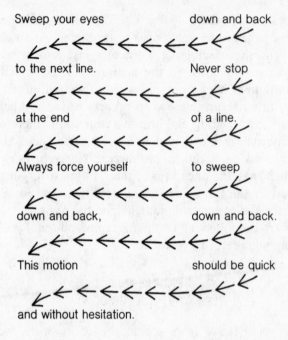

Sweep your eyes   down and back
to the next line.   Never stop
at the end   of a line.
Always force yourself   to sweep
down and back,   down and back.
This motion   should be quick
and without hesitation.

Read this next paragraph just as you read the paragraph
in the preceding exercise. There are no return arrows in
this second example, but you should still make your eyes
follow the same swift pattern that is necessary for good return eye sweep:

Pause to read.   But never pause
on the return sweep.   Move quickly, smoothly.
A reader must practice   a smooth return sweep.
A reader must practice   eliminating regressions.
A reader must practice   wide recognition spans.
Did your eyes reach   their destination
on every line?

Practice your return sweep. Use the narrow columns on the front page of any newspaper or magazine. As you read, make yourself conscious of a smooth, fast return motion; sweep back and down to the next line. Time is critical. This movement must be rapid with no wasted effort. The correct, rapid return-eye-sweep process can easily help to speed up your reading and improve your comprehension as well. One reader I had in a university class could almost daydream on each return eye sweep. Her return sweeps were such that she once said to me, "I almost forget what I've read by the time I get to the next line." So for Sally, the return-eye-sweep technique helped the most.

Now try the following two paragraphs and see if you can speed up your return eye sweep:

READING #12
DUEL AT THE SUPER BOWL

About ten or twelve years ago, most people probably thought "Super Bowl" was the name of a salad or some kind of dessert or a punch bowl. Now, Super Bowl XII is referred to as the greatest pro football game ever. The game in 1979 between the Pittsburgh Steelers and the Dallas Cowboys was played in Miami, Florida, on a Sunday afternoon in mid-January. The game highlighted the careers of two outstanding quarterbacks: Terry Bradshaw for Pittsburgh and Roger Staubach for Dallas. It was the NFL versus the AFC for the World Championship. The winner was the Pittsburgh Steelers in a dramatic, hard-fought 35–31 victory. It was the third Super Bowl victory for Pittsburgh, and that's a record in itself, for no other club has won three Super Bowls!

Mark the following statements either True (T), False (F), or Not Mentioned (N).

1. "Super Bowl" refers to the championship playoff between the NFL and AFC league champs. _____
2. Super Bowl XII was played in mid-January 1979 in Miami, Florida. _____
3. The contest was waged between the Pittsburgh Steelers and the Dallas Cowboys. _____
4. The Steelers won 35–31. _____
5. For Pittsburgh, it was their third Super Bowl victory. _____

Time/Sec.	10	12	15	20	25	30	35
WPM	846	705	564	423	338	282	241

If your time isn't shown above, divide the number of seconds it took you to read the story into 8460. That will give you your exact WPM. (For answers, see page 146.)

Place your scores beside the Reading #12 column on the Progress Chart.

READING #13
THE NEED FOR BETTER READING SKILLS

The mysteries of higher mathematics with all its complex formulas and theorems cannot be mastered or even approached until one has mastered basic addition, subtraction, multiplication, and division. In fact, most people would want more familiarity with the fundamentals of math than just how to add and subtract and would try maybe algebra or geometry before tackling calculus. However, we frequently find people trying to read from the printed page before they have mastered the basic fundamentals in the reading process. The easy and effective use of a complex skill such as speed reading or higher math comes only after a mastery of the knowledge of the fundamentals upon which the skill is based.

Mark the following statements either True (T), False (F), or Not Mentioned (N).

1. Simple arithmetic should precede complex theorems. _____
2. Effective speed reading can be mastered by anyone. _____
3. Speed reading has certain fundamentals just like math. _____
4. Reading is seldom attempted without adequate preparation. _____
5. Fundamentals aren't really essential in skill mastery. _____

Time/Sec.	5	10	15	20	25	30
WPM	1452	726	484	363	290	242

If your time isn't shown, divide into 7260 for your exact WPM. Be sure you're recording all your comprehension and WPM scores in the appropriate spaces on the Progress Chart, on page 143. (For answers, see page 146.)

FIXATIONS

The next eye movement is called a *fixation*. Fixations are the stops or pauses between eye spans. When you read, your eyes move in jumps. They fix upon a part of a line, make a hop, pause for an instant, hop again, and then the whole process is repeated. This process occurs line after line and page after page. Watch another person's eyes while he is reading. You will see him chew up a line of type in separate bites, somewhat like eating corn on the cob. This describes the basic reading procedure followed by most people. It is a series of movements and stops.

The stop, or pause, during which the eyes are momentarily at rest, is called a *fixation*. Scientists tell us that during the reading process this is the only time that vision is registered. In the quick motion between pauses, eyes do not register. To the reader, however, the eyes seem to be in continuous motion.

Reading would be a slow, awkward process if the eyes did not see and register like lightning so that everything seems to be in continuous motion. In reading, eyes function like a motion-picture camera. The eyes capture a series of printed symbols with such rapidity that these symbols are blended into what seems like a series of continuous visual impressions that convey the author's thoughts to the reader. That's why slow-motion pictures are fun to watch for a little while or periodically; they are unusual and so slow, so unnatural, that we react by laughing because we know they are exaggerated or unreal. However, viewing slow-motion pictures for any length of time soon becomes boring. Our mind starts to wander. We begin to think of other things. So it is in the reading process. We have to read at a good rate without long stops or fixations or our mind will being to daydream or wander from what we are reading. Sometimes we refer to this lapse as a lack of concentration when, actually, lengthy fixations are to blame.

Thus, *reducing the length of time required for each fixation and then reducing the number of fixations are the next steps on our improvement list.* The eyes can actually change their *fixation performance* in two ways: They can change the length of time for each fixation and they can reduce the number of fixations. For example, your eyes right now hop along this line in a pattern which you can consciously direct. You can make your eyes distinguish each letter or word if you wish. You can make your eyes fix on one letter or one word. The number of stops your eyes make and how long your eyes are stopped are the two keys in the fixation procedure. Think of a pit stop in auto racing. Periodically, every car has to make one. The number of stops and the length of each stop have a lot to do with a racer's overall speed and whether or not he wins. This is also true in speed reading. Too many or too long pit stops or fixations will mean you lose the race for speed, or WPM.

Let's try working with the fixation pauses in the following sentences. This will give you practice in examining your stop-and-go eye movements that we call fixations. Read these phrases very quickly and *focus on each dot* as briefly as you can. When you have finished the paragraph take the quiz that follows.

●
As you read   ● try to push   ● your eyes ahead.
●
Your eyes   ● stop-and-go,   ● stop-and-go
      ●
across the line.   ● Each "go" movement   ● is very fast;
●
it is merely   ● a quick dart.   ● Your eyes read
●
one each stop.   ● Make each stop   ● as short
●
as possible.   ● Do not linger   ● on any word.

Choose the word that completes each statement correctly.

1. You should not linger on any (a) idea, (b) sentence, (c) word.
2. Each "go" movement is a (a) pause, (b) dart, (c) stop.

Here are some examples which are actual replications of the basic eye movements made by three adults as each one of them read the same line of print. The vertical lines represent the points at which their eyes rested or fixed as they moved across the line. The numbers at the top of the vertical lines represent the order in which the fixations took place. The numbers at the bottom of the vertical lines represent the length of time for each fixation (measured in sixteenths of a second).

```
 1          2              3
The time is now for all good men to come to the . . .
 9          7              5

  1    2       3       5   4   6         7
The time is now for all good men to come to the . . .
  6    9       6       6   8   7         9

 1  2   4   3   5    7    6     8    10 9
The time is now for all good men to come to the . . .
30  2   18  5   6    4    10    12   26 4
```

Notice the sequence of fixations for the first reader. It was 1–2–3 right in a row. But look at the second reader who went 1–2–3–5–4. This sequence shows a regression. Now look at the third reader. Notice how long the first fixation took in comparison to the second. That isn't uncommon, because the first fixation in a line often takes longer. Note the length of the fourth fixation compared to the third. This isn't uncommon because fixations made during regressions are almost always longer than those made as you read along going forward. Think how much faster this third reader would be if he did two things about his fixations: (1) reduced the number of fixations he made and (2) reduced how long his eyes fixed at one time. His reading speed would immediately be much faster; his comprehension would also be improved since his thought processes would be more rapid and continuous. Fragmented reading due to long fixations is like listening to someone who stutters; comprehension is difficult and slow. There is no doubt that correcting these two fixation habits can really help speed up the reading process. In rapid reading it is important that the reader's fixations be of short duration and that the number of fixations not be excessive. If you cultivate the habit of rapidly picking up one thought after another and *do not make the common mistake of stopping or fixing upon each punctuation mark, your reading speed will be much faster.*

I remember as an elementary-school principal one day observing a primary teacher who said to the children: "A period means stop. You should come to a complete halt and rest the eyes on that punctuation mark we call a period. Count to yourself 1–2–3 every time you see a period and then you can go on to the next sentence." Well, I have news for that teacher; a period doesn't mean stop. A period is just a little tool or symbol we use to separate one thought from another. A sentence is usually defined as a complete thought; so as long as young readers don't have difficulty running the thoughts or sentences together, the teacher should not slow down their reading speed by teaching them to fixate for long periods of time and thus make reading a tiring and cumbersome task. Reading can be fun and rapid. Those fixations that you do make should be brief and fast-moving. Both speed and comprehension are improved by mastering this one step.

Apply this newest technique to the following paragraph. Make as few fixations as possible. Make your eyes zip right along. When you feel them stop momentarily, get them going again and keep them going. Be sure to time yourself and use the standard procedure we've been using to track your progress.

READING #14
INFLATION KILLS THE $25 U.S. SAVINGS BOND

The $25 U.S. Savings Bond was pronounced dead this year and another American tradition fell to what is rapidly becoming public enemy number one—inflation. The $25 bond had been around since World War II. But like the 5¢ candy bar, the 25¢ shoe shine and the 10¢ phone call, all good things must come to an end.

It was in 1941 when Hitler was preparing to invade Russia that the first buyer anted up the $18.75 and bought the first $25 Series E bond. By 1978, approximately 6.8 billion dollars in bonds had been sold. Sales had held steady over the years. I can remember saving pennies and nickels to buy those bonds. Now, inflation has made them a bad investment. So the Treasury officials came up with the $50 bond. It's just another sign of changing times, changing America and never-changing inflation.

Mark the following statements either True (T), False (F), or Not Mentioned (N). Put your scores in the back as usual and keep watching your progress.

1. The first U.S. Savings Bond was started in World War I.
   _____

2. The first savings bond sold for $18.75. _____
3. Bonds are redeemable in 5 years. _____
4. The new savings bond is a $50 one. _____
5. The Series F bond was the type discontinued. _____

Time/Sec.	5	10	12	15	20	25	30	35
WPM	1872	936	780	624	468	374	312	267

If your time isn't shown, divide the number of seconds it took you to read the paragraph into 9360 for your exact WPM. (For answers, see page 146.)

The paragraph you have just read is different from all the preceding ones in this book in one major aspect, which is why it was placed here: It has a lot of numbers in it. Perhaps you didn't notice that. Perhaps you hadn't noticed that all the previous paragraphs and readings contained very few numbers. The reason for this is quite simple: Reading numbers requires the reader to make more fixations than reading words does. This is why whenever we are reading along and suddenly encounter a date or number, we make a long fixation at that point. We kind of burn the number into our memory, and this is all a part of the fixation process. Whenever you see numbers, be aware of the fixations you make and how they affect your reading rate.

To understand why we fixate more on numbers than words, we have to understand *configuration*. In the world of reading, configuration refers to the distinct size and shape of a word. Take the word "good." It has a distinct size and shape (or configuration).

There are very few other words that have the very same configuration. In essence, as we grow older and gain experience in reading and have seen the same word many times, we cease to read the word closely and recognize it by its configuration. Try to figure out the following sentence by configuration. I'll give you a few helpful hints by placing some letters throughout the sentence to aid you in deciphering it.

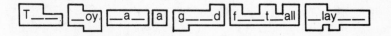

Figure it out? If you did, you read it by configuration. We all do this everyday. If you've been driving for a long time you don't "read" the stop signs in the same manner you did as when you first learned to drive. You read them by configuration. You see the shape of the sign and know what it says. The sentence above says: "The boy was a good football player."

It might surprise you to learn that numbers, unlike words, have very little configuration. It's because of this that numbers are harder to read and require more fixations. In fact, that's what prompted an old friend of mine to call me this past week. Dick is a CPA. He said it wasn't unusual for him to take several hours to read the paper in the evening. He wanted to take a speed-reading course and asked where he could find such a class offered.

Dick's reading style grew out of his habit of fixing on numbers every day in his work. Accuracy for an accountant is critical. However, he carried over his fixation reading habit into his leisure, or pleasure, reading. Many people who deal with figures every day—bankers, accountants, stockbrokers, and insurance agents—tend to lengthy fixations in their reading style.

Try to read the following series of numbers and you'll see how many more fixations it takes to read numbers. Read each line across in a horizontal manner, left to right:

NUMBER EXERCISE

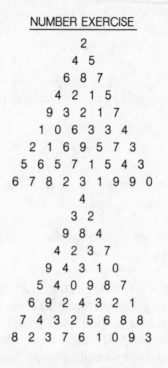

```
                2
              4 5
            6 8 7
          4 2 1 5
        9 3 2 1 7
      1 0 6 3 3 4
    2 1 6 9 5 7 3
  5 6 5 7 1 5 4 3
6 7 8 2 3 1 9 9 0
                4
              3 2
            9 8 4
          4 2 3 7
        9 4 3 1 0
      5 4 0 9 8 7
    6 9 2 4 3 2 1
  7 4 3 2 5 6 8 8
8 2 3 7 6 1 0 9 3
```

If you were aware of your eye movements as you read those numbers, you would have noticed that after you reached four numbers in a row, you were making fixations on at least every two or three numbers per line. You must have also noticed that you couldn't read numbers by configuration. Look at the next to last set of numbers. It has no distinct configuration compared to a word. The word "educated" has eight letters instead of eight digits as in the next to last set of numbers. Yet it is much easier to read and remember "educated" than 74325688.

Now try the following paragraph which contains no numbers. *Go for speed.* You will notice how much easier it is to read because there are no numbers. See how your reading speed on this paragraph compares to #14 with all the figures and numbers. You should be able to read this next paragraph at a much faster rate.

READING #15
MANKIND'S NEED FOR ENERGY

For the foreseeable future, no one form of energy can meet all our needs. We don't have enough domestic petroleum; and coal can't power cars. At least not yet. Nuclear or solar energy, at least in this century, can't generate all our electricity needs. So the energy we need must come from a combination of sources. The key to meeting today's energy needs is a variety of energy sources—oil, solar, natural gas, coal and uranium. Perhaps alternative fuels will also be developed more fully. Because mankind needs so much energy and needs it now, we will need to look to a variety of energy sources.

Mark the following statements either True (T), False (F), or Not Mentioned (N).

1. We will have an unending supply of energy. _____
2. Solar and nuclear energy will supply all our electrical needs.

   _____
3. The energy we need must come from a combination of sources. _____
4. A new energy fuel has been discovered. _____
5. The federal government is subsidizing research on energy sources. _____

Time/Sec.	2	5	10
WPM	3390	1356	678

If your time isn't shown above, divide the seconds into 6780 for your WPM. (For answers, see page 147.)

7

Improving Your Comprehension and Retention

Comprehension is the art of understanding what you read. Retention is what you retain or remember from that initial understanding. Comprehension is probably the most misunderstood aspect of reading because it is so unlike speed, which can basically be attributed to eye movements. Eye patterns can be seen, studied, and understood. They are visible. Comprehension, on the other hand, is invisible and mysterious. You can't trace or see it. Even definitions and explanations of comprehension often disagree. In my opinion, comprehension is simply the understanding we receive when we read something. Comprehension is the other half of the reading process; speed, or rate, is the first half. We learn to move our eyes over the printed page in a certain way; the result is meaning. If you don't move your eyes properly, you reduce your comprehension. Thus, rate is the first essential factor; comprehension comes next as the product of this effort. Comprehension doesn't have to be mysterious. It can be improved if you go about it properly.

Comprehension in reading can be compared to accuracy in typing or style in swimming. In the development of all three of these skills, you must first get the speed where you want it and then work on fine points of accuracy, style, or comprehension, as the case may be. If you're trying to be a good typist, you push your speed up until you are satisfied and then you work on accuracy. In swimming you first get to the other end of the pool in the time desired, then you begin to concentrate on improving style, stroke, or positioning of the head, shoulders, etc. Likewise with reading, which brings us to the basic question of this chapter: *How can comprehension be improved?* Here are the steps you should inculcate into your reading if you are to develop outstanding comprehension skills.

First, *attention* is an absolute prerequisite to intensive mental impressions. Impressions from the printed page are the essence of comprehension. In fact, the intensity of the original impression is proportionate to the attention given the item to be remembered. In other words, the more attention you pay to something, the stronger the mental impression you will receive.

What is attention? It is the will to direct the intellect into some particular channel and keep it there. It is mind over matter. What does that mean to you in terms of improving your ability to remember what you read? It means that you must give your undivided attention to what you want to recall. You must *will* to fix vividly in your subconscious mind whatever you mean to remember. Your memory awaits your commands. The human mind is a powerhouse of untapped energy.

The next factor is *interest*. Interest is very important. We always give voluntary attention to anything we are interested in. A musician may give a lot of attention to a musical rendition by a great master but may have great difficulty in giving attention to a lecture on basketball. Interest is an indication of our values and priorities.

So it is with reading. If you are deeply interested in the

content of a selection, you probably won't have to concern yourself about giving attention or about recalling the author's ideas later. You dig right into the reading. You get involved with the author's thoughts.

The third point in improving comprehension is *purpose*. Most of the reading people do is not the result of a compelling interest. It is either because they are required to read the material or feel they have to, because it is related to work, school, college, etc. I would say leisure reading is a small part of the amount of actual reading the average person does today. So our purpose in reading plays an important part in the amount of comprehension we receive and retain. Take, for example, the evening newspaper. Most people read through it and a day later can't remember much (if anything) about what they read. Their purpose in reading did not require a high degree of recall.

Purpose contributes greatly to the amount of attention we spend on certain readings. If we just wander through an article with no purpose in mind, we do not bring strong attention to bear on the subject. On the other hand, if we have a definite purpose, we focus attention on whatever will fulfill this need within us. That's the way people are. If they are interested, they pay attention. Interest together with purpose constitute a perfect team. Without interest, you must draw strongly upon your purpose and reserves of willpower to make your attention strong enough to result in vivid impressions. When you're reading for purpose, ask yourself questions as you go along, such as those on page 73.

The fourth point on the road to better comprehension is *concentration*. Concentration is the process of holding your attention long enough to establish the vivid impressions which contribute so much to recall abilities. The power of

concentrating attention on what you read breaks down into two components: exclusion of extraneous or unnecessary data and *staying on the track*. Exclusion means the ability to shut out *all* sights, sounds, and thoughts except the one on which you wish to concentrate, thus giving one hundred percent of your attention to the reading's content. Divided attention won't yield a vivid impression or good comprehension. Thinking about next weekend's big event is not the way to concentrate and have good comprehension on what you are reading. If, when focusing your attention on information that you wish to remember, you can become absolutely oblivious to everything else in the world, then you will receive the strongest possible impression your mind can absorb.

Association is another great factor in recall and comprehension. A natural, rational association of ideas is a very useful way to fix ideas in one's mind for later retention or recall. The development of word association should improve your ability to recall what you read. In word association, ideas are assimilated on the basis of their relatedness, and any one idea in a chain of related ideas helps to recall the others that belong with it. Thus, the person who is trying to recall has several "handles" to take hold of in calling forth any set of related facts or ideas which he has impressed upon his mind through previous reading. For example, summer: swimming, sunbathing, vacations, picnics, golf, hot, barbecues, Fourth of July. Another example would be war: guns, uniforms, battles, rations, planes, jeeps, ships, tanks, etc. The reader associates one word with another or with a series of other words in accordance with experience.

Repetition is another technique that improves comprehension. Briefly stated: All other things being equal, the intensity of an impression can be increased by *repeatedly* reviewing it. Studies on comprehension show that the first time a person reads something his comprehension usually ranges from 40 to 60 percent. The second time he reads the same material, there is a significant increase in comprehension. And the third time he reads the same material there is still some further increase in comprehension.

Distributed practice is highly effective in improving comprehension when it is properly coupled with repetition. Experiments have shown that you are much more likely to recall what you have studied again and again at *spaced intervals* than what you have studied just once (or twice if the second reading immediately followed the first). That is why it is suggested that you begin preparing for a test several weeks ahead of the actual examination and study the same subject repeatedly at different intervals.

Use of several different senses provides a multitude of

avenues to improving your memory and comprehension skills. In studying difficult material for the first time or in reviewing for exams, just *reading* is not enough. You need to do more than cover the pages in the usual way. *Write* the subject matter down in outline form; make a summary or compile an organized list. *Say* it aloud. Underline the important passages. Write notes on the margin of the book. *Draw* diagrams or sketches to illustrate it. *Make up a test* of your own on the material, and later take the test you have made. The more things you do with the subject matter, the better your recall will be.

You will improve your ability to comprehend and retain what you have read if you follow the rules listed on page 76.

Apply these principles of better comprehension to the following paragraph and watch the results! Use the Progress Chart in the back to record your improvement.

READING # 16
LEARNING TO SPEED READ

Years of teaching speed reading have led me to conclude that the average person can learn to read from 400 to 500 words per minute. It is not uncommon to see people learn to speed read at 1,200 to 1,500 words per minute or even higher, with comprehension that is just as good as they had when reading at their earlier slow rate. Such results many be achieved almost immediately in some cases; in two, three, and four weeks of intensive practice at 20 minutes per day for others. Sometimes up to ten to twelve weeks are needed to achieve the high reading rate desired. Such improvements in reading speed and comprehension are due, in part, to the fact that many of us do not use our mental abilities to the fullest. The mental potential and energies we all have are unbelievably powerful and can be brought into action by our desire to improve.

READING POWER

KNOW EXACTLY WHY . . .

you are reading a story. Ask yourself what you want from the material.

LOOK FOR KEY WORDS . . .

and take notes. Use your different senses. The more senses you use, the more your comprehension will increase.

ASSOCIATE . . .

new ideas with old ones or with your experience.

CONCENTRATION AND ATTENTION

Focus on what you're reading, not on the radio or surrounding events or daydreams, etc.

REPETITION

Read the material at least twice. Then read it once again.

DISTRIBUTED PRACTICE

Read the same material at different intervals, allowing some time to lapse between each reading.

The ultimate purpose of reading is to *synthesize* the author's thoughts and your thinking, so

ANALYZE AND USE . . .

what you've learned or read as soon as you've finished. This can be accomplished by putting the author's message into your own words, reflecting about what you've read, and evaluating what the author said.

Mark the following statements either True (T), False (F), or Not Mentioned (N).

1. The average person can learn to read at 400 to 500 words per minute. _____
2. Some results may be expected immediately. _____
3. The desire to improve is important. _____
4. Those who learn to speed read, generally lose comprehension.
   _____
5. Learning to speed read is another part of our contemporary fast-paced life style. _____

Time/Sec.	5	7	10	12	15	17
WPM	1932	1380	966	805	644	568

If your time isn't shown, divide into 9660 for your WPM. (For answers, see page 147.)

VOCABULARY

An old argument often heard when it comes to the study of comprehension relates to vocabulary. You've probably heard the case before; it goes something like this: "I don't understand what I read because my vocabulary isn't big enough," or, "I didn't know that word, that's why I didn't understand that paragraph" or that article or page or sentence, and, "Once I build up my vocabulary, I'm going to start to read." The excuses go on ad infinitum. But if the truth were really known, no one understands *exactly* what a writer is saying with each and every word. Words have a general meaning and we understand generally what the author is trying to convey to us. Do you doubt that words usually have a general meaning for most readers? Many lawyers could make a living out of debating what certain words really mean or connote. If all words meant the same thing to all people, communication would be much easier than it is.

The best thing to do for reading ability is to read. A good vocabulary isn't built overnight, and you don't learn to read by building the vocabulary first and then learning to read faster later. You'll wind up waiting forever if you use that logic. A good vocabulary is the result of reading, not vice versa. So if you want a large vocabulary, start to read and keep at it. You'll soon develop a bigger and better vocabulary.

EYE MOVEMENTS AND COMPREHENSION

Up to now, you have learned a great deal about the eye movements made in reading. Our emphasis has been on ways to improve these movements. You may have read or heard that this kind of approach causes a loss in comprehension; the argument basically goes like this: Poor eye movements are a result of poor reading, and if we read better our eye movements will be better. This is like telling a man that he'll be a better husband and father if he gets along with his wife and kids. That kind of thinking doesn't tell the husband what he should do specifically to be a better husband or father. Advice-givers who think like this would probably respond, "We told you that you should be a better husband—or a better reader. Now you figure it out."

People need to be told specific techniques on how to be better readers (or better partners). If we really want someone to learn something we show them by examples and concrete, step-by-step methods. That's basically what this book does when it demonstrates techniques like a good, wide eye span, no regressions, short fixations, etc. Compare this kind of specific know-how to advice like "read faster."

What's more, this whole debate is really a moot point, for comprehension initially always lags behind when any change is made in one's reading style. The mind has to readjust to the tempo at which it is being fed. It is used to receiving, sorting, and interpreting data at a certain rate of speed. Any sudden change means the mind has to re-acclimate to receiving data at a new faster rate. We call this *comprehension lag*. In the field of speed reading, it usually takes ten to fifteen days for the mind to acclimate to the new reading rate. It is virtually impossible to improve the reading speed and the comprehension at the very same time. One must come first. The lag process works like this:

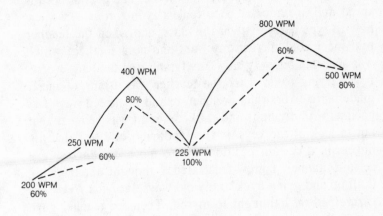

Note that the reader started at 200 WPM with 60 percent comprehension. After practice over several weeks he is able to read at 500 WPM with 80 percent comprehension. Once the mind adjusts to the new rate at which data is fed to it along with the increased concentration applied by the reader who is reading faster, comprehension is better than ever.

Comprehension is dependent on a host of variables such as level of difficulty of the material being read, the purpose in reading the material, the speed at which it is being read and how new that level of speed is to the reader, and the reader's physiological and psychological condition. If the reader's mind has experienced the feeling of reading at that speed before and has grown fairly comfortable with it, then comprehension will be better than ever. Practice is needed for ten to fifteen days while one changes old habits and learns new ones. As I said earlier, learning to speed read is very much like learning to type. The goal of both is speed and accuracy. I once took a typing course. I knew how to type before I took the class, and when the teacher told me I couldn't use my hunt-and-peck method, which was accurate but very slow, my typing was suddenly worse. I was trying to do what the teacher was asking of me. I made more errors than ever before and my speed wasn't as good as with my hunt-and-peck system. I was being taught not to look at the keys on the typewriter and to place my fingers in a certain position and to move my fingers in a certain manner. I grew frustrated. I thought about giving it all up and going back to my old ways. *At least I was accurate before,* I thought to myself. Then the teacher gave me some simple advice: *"Hang in there."* For some reason I did. My speed gradually became better and better as I practiced more and more. Soon the new ways became familiar to me and I could hardly recall the old habits. The adjustment period was over. My typing was faster and more accurate.

In speed reading, the sequence works the same way. At first you think your accuracy or comprehension is worse than ever and you debate whether or not you should continue with your efforts to master this new skill. It is easy to give in to temptation and talk yourself into being satisfied with slow speed in reading. The eye movements being taught to you through this book are new to you. Give them a chance. Practice them. The end result will be a better reading rate and much more comprehension! Just remember and compare the process to learning to type. Relearning a skill is always harder than learning it the first time. Changing how you read is harder than learning to read for the first time. This is so because you have to *unlearn* the old ways in order to learn the new.

Another argument on comprehension says that if you concentrate on specific techniques (no matter what techniques they are), you will give most or all of your attention to those techniques instead of concentrating on the author's message. If you examine that logic closely, you'll see it's like telling an athlete to forget working and practicing on all the specific techniques taught by the coach and just think about being a superstar. Teams and individuals succeed and excel because they pay a great deal of attention to the little mechanics, steps, and procedures. They work at them over and over again until they master them completely. That's what being a professional means. So it is with reading. This book tells you the specifics. It tells you precise techniques which will make you a better reader: for example, *shorten your fixation time, broaden your eye span, read in thought units, don't regress, always push forward, vary the rate, quicken your recognition rate,* etc.

You know as well as I do, and common sense dictates, that to speed read or to improve your reading takes more than the mere desire to pick up a book and read better and faster. It is through the actual, little step-by-step methods and hours of practice that people master anything in life. It is through such specifics and hard work that success and concentration are achieved. These ingredients are necessary for any worthwhile accomplishment.

The formula I am prescribing works like this:

$$RR = MC = MC = MR$$

The letters in the formula above stand for:

Rapid Reading	=	More Concentration	=	More Comprehension	=	More Retention

Here's the logic. If you start with step 1 (rapid reading) you are forced to concentrate and pay attention. You have no time to daydream and let your mind wander. You are reading a little faster than your normal slow rate and this leads us to step 2—more concentration. You are forced to concentrate more because you are reading faster. Simple, but true. Step 3—more concentration means more comprehension! After all, isn't this what people say: "If I could only concentrate more, I'd get more out of what I read." Thus, if a reader concentrates more, it is logical that he will retain more (which is the fourth step). The formula can be summarized like this: You learn the specific steps of fast reading and thus begin to read faster; the increased rate makes you more attentive and you concentrate more; the greater concentration is rewarded by better comprehension; the better comprehension in turn gives you more retention. That's the way it is. Don't let comprehension be a roadblock for you. There are certain obstacles that hinder reading speed. We know how to correct these, and you can already see the results of your efforts. Continue concentrating on learning the specific steps, and you'll see your reading speed and comprehension both improve. Check your progress to date in the back of the book as proof of your newfound success.

Try these next two paragraphs and remember . . . SPEED . . . SPEED!

READING # 17
READING SPEED'S EFFECT ON COMPREHENSION

Some people believe that if they read too fast their comprehension will suffer. However, research shows that as you learn to read rapidly, comprehension may be even better than it was before. Such improvement generally is attributed to the fact that the more rapidly you read, the more you must concentrate on what is being read. Therefore, you comprehend more. Comprehension may be lower for a short time when you first attempt to speed read, but comprehension almost always improves when speed is gained.

Mark the following statements True (T), False (F), or Not Mentioned (N).

1. Comprehension may suffer when you first attempt speed reading. _____
2. Poor vision is a factor to be considered when learning to speed read. _____
3. Comprehension improves when speed is gained. _____
4. Skipping, scanning and skimming are techniques used in speed reading. _____
5. One reason why comprehension improves when speed is gained is increased concentration. _____

Time/Sec.	3	5	7	10	12
WPM	1840	1104	789	552	460

Divide into 5520 for your WPM if your time isn't shown. (For answers, see page 147.)

READING #18
THIS BOOK

You can put this book to work every day of the year and put an end to slow, sluggish reading habits that cost you hours of enjoyment and leisure time. This book shows you how to speed read and cut hours off your reading time for all types of reading. This book shows you how to eliminate all those wasteful, time-consuming reading habits and replace them with successful new how-to-do-it speed-reading techniques. All across America, you'll find people using this book to train themselves to speed read. This book will save you more than its price the first day you use it because your time is worth money!

Mark the following statements True (T), False (F), or Not Mentioned (N).

1. This book will save you money. _____
2. This book will show you how to sight read. _____
3. This book can cut hours off your reading time. _____
4. This book shows you how to speed read. _____
5. This book is a "how-to" book. _____

Time/Sec.	3	5	7	10	12
WPM	2360	1416	1011	708	590

Divide into 7080 for your WPM if your time isn't shown. (For answers, see page 147.)

8

Improving Your Recognition Rate

Your *recognition rate* is the rate at which you see and understand what you read. A more technical definition for this new term might be "the rate at which you see and understand the symbols on the printed page." We generally refer to this process as reading. Your *recognition rate* is one of the most basic factors that must be taken into account if you are going to be a speed reader. The reason for this is actually quite simple: A slow recognition rate usually means that the reader is having difficulty recognizing the words and this results in a slow reading speed. We are assuming here, of course, that the reader has normal vision or is wearing some type of corrective lens to give normal vision. Fatigue is a common factor experienced by readers who have a slow recognition rate. For them, reading is a sluggish, painful process. They get a headache or their eyes become tired or their vision grows blurred after twenty or thirty minutes of reading. Thus, readers with a slow recognition rate seldom sit down to read for any long periods of time. They can blame many things for their slow reading style such as boring or dull subject matter, limited vocabulary, eye strain, lack of concentration, or the mysterious sudden headaches they say they get so easily when they read.

Sometimes the recognition rate is called your *page-response rate.* Another way to put it is, how fast you think or react to what you see. Sometimes it is called your *rate of perception.* In essence, it is how fast you recognize and process what you are reading. A slow recognition rate causes a slow reading speed. Staring at the word(s) on the page for a few seconds longer lowers your WPM without increasing comprehension. In addition, slow recognition rate often encourages regressions. So now there are three variables that can reduce your reading effectiveness: a slow recognition rate, too many long fixations, and regressions. These three factors have nothing to do with IQ, motivation or vocabulary.

You might now ask how are you to learn new words and build a good vocabulary if you don't stop and examine new words? Vocabulary development was discussed in more detail in chapter 7, but now the point should be made that though *recognition rate* is admittedly slow on new words it should not be slow on all the other words. Since most people know most of the words they read each day, recognition rate should not be a problem. The only reason it is is because most people haven't worked at improving it. You can train your recognition rate and that training will make you a faster and better reader.

An important point to keep in mind is that recognition rate is learned at a young age. It is very common for young children to stumble along with uncertainty in their reading, especially when new words are continually being introduced to them. Thus, it is easy to develop a slow recognition rate which is applied to all words, new or old. Sometimes this problem is referred to as *lazy eyes,* but your eyes will be lazy only if you let them. If you are a fast reader, your recognition rate is rapid, with no long stares of uncertainty. During the recognition phase, you quickly and effortlessly recognize a word or group of words as well as immediately understand the meaning associated with the word(s). Because this process is so quick, your reading speed is very fast. Your comprehension or understanding is equally rapid. You read and comprehend quickly and with more understanding because your eyes and brain are instantly perceiving the author's message. Perhaps this whole process can be compared to a computer. Some computers process the data faster than others. The accuracy of the new fast computer is equal to that of the older slower model. The difference is in the processing rate. Your mind is like a computer with fantastic potential. It has the potential and the ability to process words at amazing speed. You only have to feed it faster, and you do this by reading faster.

Let's check your recognition rate, or page-response rate, by using the following test. We can utilize the results to improve your reading abilities. It should also be pointed out that this test of recognition abilities has been often used to determine recognition rates for driving tests. Yes, your recognition rate has an effect on how well you drive, in that it is some indication of how quickly you react to what you see. The following test for driving tells whether your reaction speed qualifies you to drive over 45 mph. In the case of speed reading, it tells how your recognition rate, or page-response rate, compares to that of thousands of others who have taken the same test. The directions are simple: See how fast you can identify the twelve numerals in the twelve squares in the proper sequence, or numerical order. Touch each number with the index finger as you read it. Check your time in seconds. See how long it takes you to do this. Ready? Remember, you must touch each number in sequence. Go!

4	3	10	12
6	11	8	9
1	7	2	5

How did you come out? Within nine seconds? Your reactions and eye span are about average. Within seven seconds? Very good. Within six or five? Excellent! If your time was longer than nine seconds, your reactions are too slow, and you had better not drive over 45 mph. You should work at improving your recognition rate, which will improve your reading speed as well as enable you to react more quickly to unexpected driving factors such as those interstate highway signs that are so easy to miss. It is a slow recognition rate and too many fixations that cause people to miss those signs. If they had time, they could easily read them accurately and correctly The frustration of a slow recognition rate is obvious when the driver says something to the effect: "Darn, I missed that sign. Did you see what it said? I couldn't finish it; I saw the name of the city, but how many miles was that?" Or maybe, "What route was that?" or, "How many miles was it to that exit?"

INCREASING THE RATE

An excellent way to increase visual perception is through drill on the mechanical aspects of quickly recognizing words on the page. This can be done with machines, which will be discussed in chapter 11, but right now probably the only reason your recognition rate isn't faster is because you've never seriously pushed it to be faster. You've told yourself that stepping up your recognition rate only results in confusion or lack of comprehension, so you should be satisfied with your present level. You've wanted to increase your reading speed but haven't known how. Well, now you do. From now on, the only thing that can hold you back is your own failure to put forth the effort needed to break old habits and form new ones. You can change your recognition rate by pushing yourself to read faster. *You can do it!* You can, in essence, develop new eye muscles or new eye patterns and rid yourself of *lazy eyes*. Just as in training for anything involving complex motor skills, such as athletics, it takes motivation, willpower, consistency, and practice. But perhaps the most important ingredient is desire. I can show you the techniques, but you have to put them to use, and that's where your motivation level comes in. How motivated are you? How much energy are you willing to put forth to improve your reading skills? A famous former football coach recently said, "Nothing worthwhile ever comes cheap. You give a man something and it amounts to nothing. If the price is high, sometimes a youngster isn't willing to accept the price. Then you have to push him. But it has to be done. Each man has a much greater potential than he thinks he does."

These statements all indicate that you have to push yourself to excel. "Pushing" to change your recognition rate means that you consciously move right along. You force yourself to read faster. It is important when you do this *at first* that you think about speed as well as what you are reading. If you forget about speed, you will stop reading fast because you will slip back to your old habit of reading at one slow steady speed; and if you don't think about what you are reading (to some extent) your comprehension will be so poor you will get discouraged. Thus, your primary concentration at first is on going faster and second on what the author is saying.

Apply your new, faster recognition rate to the following paragraph and see what a difference it'll make in your reading speed. Remember, go for SPEED FIRST, COMPREHENSION SECOND!

READING # 19
COMIC BOOKS COME TO HOLLYWOOD

A look at the TV shows produced by Hollywood for today's prime-time TV will reveal that many of yesterday's comic-book heroes are now today's TV superstars: There's Superman leaping over buildings at a single bound, there's Spider Man crawling up the wall, there's Wonder Woman flying in her invisible plane with her magic lasso, there's, of course, Batman and Robin bringing WOW! PIFF! ZAP! right onto the home viewer's TV screen. The latest two shows, *The Incredible Hulk* and *Captain America,* offer more superheroes to the American youth who avidly watch these entertaining shows of fantasy. Some cynics might say TV has turned into one big comic book, but the majority of the viewing audience intently watch their new favorite heroes win over the bad guys!

Mark the following statements either True (T), False (F) or Not Mentioned (N).

1. Many of yesterday's comic book heroes are now on TV.
   _____

2. Batman's archrival bad guy is called The Joker. _____
3. The newest show is *Wonder Woman.* _____
4. Some people refer to all these TV shows as today's electronic comic books. _____

5. Clark Kent is the mild-mannered reporter who is really Superman in disguise. _____

Time/Sec.	5	10	15	20	25
WPM	1740	870	580	435	348

If your time isn't shown, divide into 8700 for your
WPM. (For answers, see page 147.)

VARYING THE RATE

Another eye movement that is essential to speed reading
is called *varying the rate of speed*. This can greatly increase your words per minute. You might ask, "Just what
does varying the rate of your reading speed do?" The following example will illustrate this point and give you a better understanding of how important this skill can be. You
could probably state fairly accurately how far you drive
your car in one year. But could you state how far you
"drive" your eyes during your reading activities in a year's
time? Probably not. The chances are that your eyes travel
about 1,600 feet per day in the reading process! That figure, which applies to most adults, amounts to approximately 584,000 feet per year or about 110 miles or 177 kilome-
ters. If you are a high-school, college, or graduate student,
these figures could easily be more than doubled. Could you
imagine traveling 110 or 220 miles in a car at one slow
constant speed? Or traveling 110 miles at say, 20 miles per
hour, with periodic long stops between exits and frequent
backing up as you travel along trying to make your way to
another city? Ridiculous, you might say. Yes—but that's
the way some people read, and their goal is similar to driving a car: Their objective is to get to a predetermined
point. The driver's goal may be a distant city or another

state, while the reader's goal is to finish a page or a chapter. Both the driver and the reader need to push forward at varying rates according to the circumstances and conditions they face.

The point is, of course, that readers should vary their reading speed just as people do when they drive at different rates of speed. Reading speed should be geared to different variables such as the purpose in reading the particular selection, the level of difficulty of the selection, the type and style of the author and text, and the familiarity of the material. Varying the rate of speed in reading allows you to be more selective in the application of your energies to the words. Why apply your energy in an equal fashion to all words? Ask yourself if each word is of equal value in its meaning. Is each word of equal importance in its relationship to the message of the author? Obviously not. So then a reader's energies should be applied proportionately.

Increased mental alertness, an overall higher average reading speed, and better comprehension are by products of varying the rate of your reading speed. In achieving this goal, do not become "hung up," as many readers do, by only reading in horizontal line patterns. Develop some rapid vertical eye movements in your reading process just as in reading the front page of a newspaper. Get into the author's style, purpose, and format. Allow your eyes to flow ahead or scan the page before and after you read it. Pick up key words or lead sentences. Look for *go-ahead* signals which can help speed up your reading. Words such as "for example," and "for instance," indicate to the reader that similar or substantiating thoughts are about to follow. If you already understand the author's thought, you may want to skip the example. Caution signals like "however," "but," "although," and "on the other hand" should indicate a reduction in the reader's speed—or at least that some increased concentration is due on the point that is about to follow. These go-ahead signs and caution signals indicate the thought pattern of the writer, and you would do well to heed them.

The eyes are really servants of the mind and should do its bidding in the reading process, just as the hands do the bidding of the mind when told to "throw the ball" or "pick up the book." You can work on the process of varying the reading rate as you read any material. It is applicable to all levels of reading from highly technical material to easy leisure reading.

What does varying the rate of speed actually do? It: (1) increases mental awareness, (2) utilizes energy in a more efficient manner, (3) places concentration power where it is needed, (4) increases overall reading speed, and (5) helps to build and maintain better comprehension levels.

Here's how varying the rate accomplishes these things:

Accelerated rate

VARYING THE RATE = a higher overall average rate.

Normal rate

As you can see, the overall rate or WPM is much faster if a reader periodically varies the rate. He or she can read the more important messages very slowly and thoroughly while pushing the reading speed rapidly over lesser points. The end result is to double the reading speed. In addition, comprehension is improved by concentrating mental energies where they do the most good: on the author's main points.

Here's how a reading speed profile would normally look

before an individual has taken a course in speed reading or read this book.

| 200 WPM | 200 WPM | 200 WPM |

Let's utilize the technique of varying the rate on the following story and see what it does to your words per minute. Read the article twice. The first time read it at your normal rate, but keep track of the number of seconds it takes you to read the selection. On the second time, vary the rate. Hit your very highest and fastest rate and hold it up there for a while. Keep track of the number of seconds it takes you to complete this second reading too. Then compare the two rates and see what a difference this new skill makes. Your comprehension should be outstanding because you're focusing on the important words and key phrases. Give it a try now. Go!

THE AMERICAN EAGLE

The American bald eagle was once abundant throughout the southwestern United States where there are large bodies of water that provide the fish which are such an important item of its diet. Constant persecution by hunters and egg collectors has greatly reduced the numbers of the bald eagle, but in the wilder portions of its range it is still abundant. During the winter months the bald eagle is even seen near New York City, though probably it does not breed within many miles of there. It now enjoys the full protection of the law and seems to be slowly increasing its numbers.

The bald eagle is most adept at the capture of fish. At times it may take its prey in a spectacular swoop from the blue, at other times it may be seen wading in shallow water, watchful for venturesome victims. But skillful though it may be in plying its trade, it is no match for that consummate fisherman, the osprey eagle. It is common practice for the more powerful bald eagle to assume the role of bandit and to rob the weaker osprey of its catch. Having watched a successful dive on the part of its rival, the eagle rushes to the attack with a great show of fierceness. This alarms the osprey so that in order to make certain of escaping its tormentor, it releases its clutch on its burden and speeds away on frightened wings. The pirate is then free to seize the fish as it falls or to retrieve it at leisure from the surface of the water.

Fish do not form the sole diet of the bald eagle. When necessity arises, it is surprisingly swift on the wing, and in localities where wild ducks are abundant the eagle is perfectly capable of capturing them in full flight. Small mammals or rodents are also taken on occasion.

In flight the bald eagle is truly magnificent. With wings spread wide, floating with hardly perceptible efforts, it glides through the air with an ease and grace which no manmade machine has ever equaled. Aided by favorable air currents, it rises to tremendous heights, swinging in great circles, often beyond the vision of the human eye.

A few years ago, I had a remarkable view of the grandiosity of the bald eagle in flight. Driving along a turnpike in Pennsylvania, I suddenly spotted a moving spot of white. And there, sailing smoothly on outstretched wings, in full regalia of pure white head and tail, was the superb American bald eagle. His nearly motionless ease gave a false impression of his speed; for while I gazed spellbound he passed out of sight. The rays of reflected sunlight scintillated from his outstretched wings.

In 1974 a national wildlife study showed there were 500 bald eagles born in the United States; and of these, four were born in my native state of Ohio. Let's do our share to help preserve these birds as part of our heritage and do our part in the conservation of nature.

Divide your time (seconds) into 39,000 (the estimated word count for the reading selection) and that will give you your WPM. You should be faster on this reading than any reading completed yet (if you truly varied your reading rate and did not slip back into the old habit of reading word-by-word at one slow steady speed). You are breaking some lifetime habits and it may take a while; you just have to remember to keep at it.

Before we leave this chapter, let's apply varying the rate to the following paragraph. Record your speed and comprehension scores on the Progress Chart in the back.

READING #20
READING IS A SKILL

One wouldn't expect to be born with a thorough knowledge of music or athletics. It usually takes years to develop a good musician or super athlete. For instance, most instruments require hours of practice and application. So why should we expect to have good reading skills without any effort? The answer is that we may all expect to, but we certainly won't all gain them unless we have guidance and practice of the proper kind. The average person may, by putting forth a little effort combined with techniques from this book, see immediate improvement in his or her reading speed. It is not difficult to double your reading speed, but just think what you could do if you were to practice for only a few weeks.

Mark the following statements True (T), False (F), or Not Mentioned (N).

1. Those persons with greater intelligence are most likely to have good reading skills. _____
2. Eyesight plays an important part in speed reading. _____

3. The average person, by putting forth a little effort combined with techniques from this book, can see immediate improvement.

_____

4. It usually takes years to develop good athletes and musicians.

_____

5. Speed reading cannot be compared to music or athletics.

_____

Time/Sec.	2	3	5	7	10	12
WPM	3960	2640	1584	1131	792	660

If your time isn't shown, divide into 7920 the number of seconds it took you to read this paragraph. Don't forget to keep a record of your progress in the back of this book. (For answers, see page 147.)

9

Reading Habits of
Some Famous Americans

It is interesting to consider the reading patterns of some Americans, past and present, whose positions have required them to read vast amounts of material. This, of course, is especially true of Presidents.

GEORGE WASHINGTON

It is said that Washington liked to read even when he was on horseback. He would move his lips, forming the passages he was reading and "hear the words with his inner ear," as they referred to this process back then. His reading speed was not so ferocious as was his appetite to read everything he could put his hands on. He especially liked English books on agriculture, because he considered himself a country gentleman farmer. He was a steady, consistent reader who paced himself through material without backing up and re-reading. Occasionally he would re-read an entire chapter, but he seldom regressed on one or two words.

THOMAS JEFFERSON

Jefferson believed in mapping out his reading into a definite plan of action, covering each topic in a particular way and never allowing himself to deviate from his reading schedule until it had been fully carried out. No distractions, no dissipation of time and energy by scattered inattentiveness—these are keys to understanding Jefferson's tremendous power of concentration. He also believed that one should choose a course of reading very purposefully for definite training or for needed knowledge, cultivation, or recreation. He would make a list of books in such categories to be read.

He used a clock to schedule himself precisely and always advised this method to others. "Knowing where you are, and what you are doing, and what time it is, and whether you are falling short of your schedule or not, and how far short." It is clear that this was what he made himself do in all matters and particularly in his reading. We know that this type of constant, deliberate consciousness of clocklike eye movements tends to increase speed and prevent dawdling. Jefferson's speed was always calm, even stately, like the tick of a tall mahogany clock. But it was fast, nevertheless, with no false steps, no jerks of uncertainty, no flapping over the pages. His progress was massive and real.

ABRAHAM LINCOLN

The story of Abraham Lincoln's educating himself by candlelight has become an integral part of the American folk legend. Like Benjamin Franklin, Lincoln begged or borrowed every book in sight. He was an avid reader. In his early youth there was very little chance for him to obtain any broad, cosmopolitan reading material. Later he studied his law books in great detail, sometimes reading words and whole lines over and over again. He would use his self-taught reading habits in his career as a lawyer, legislator, and President. It is said that reading for Lincoln was a relief from the constant, harrowing anxiety he often experienced during the Civil War. His reading Shakespeare's *Richard II* aloud to his family in the White House is common knowledge to Lincoln scholars. He knew in the midst of those sad, turbulent days he could turn to the literature he loved for refreshment. He used reading aloud (or even to himself) to hear the words and thus feel renewed after long hours of hard work in the President's office.

THEODORE ROOSEVELT

Teddy Roosevelt was a tireless reviewer of books and a very rapid reader. He was the "colonel of the Rough Riders" in speed reading. The amount he could read at one time would seem incredible if he had not left us some valuable hints as to his style or methods of covering such massive amounts of reading material. He never said in so many words just how fast he could read or how his rates differed on different sorts of books, but we can easily infer that he sometimes skipped and scanned materials. He varied the rate according to his purpose. On this point we have a delightful series of letters to his son Kermit about how he read Dickens: "It always interests me about Dickens to think how almost all of it was mixed up with every kind of cheap, second-rate matter . . . The wise thing to do is simply to skip the bosh and twaddle and vulgarity and untruth, and get the benefit out of the rest." Note that this advice to skip and scan and vary the rate comes from a lover of Dickens, a wise, discriminating reader, who could treasure the best. Roosevelt liked to read certain books over and over again. In fact, he has given us a list of novels which he re-read not only once but "over and over again." Here it is: *Guy Mannering, The Antiquary, Pendennis, Vanity Fair, Our Mutual Friend, Pickwick Papers.* Roosevelt has also told us that he would judge the contents of a book from the index or the table of contents or the chapter headings, all of which indicate what subject matter is included.

The most important thing to notice about Roosevelt's reading, however, is not his enormous range, so much as his free use of a whole gamut of methods for different reading purposes. He could use his fingers to pace himself on a book or read parts of it slowly or skip boldly over all other parts or read at a prodigious rate of speed or read carefully for review or read the same story over and over again.

FRANKLIN D. ROOSEVELT

FDR was probably among America's best readers of all time. He could read an entire paragraph at a single glance! He started out like everyone else—reading one then two words at a time. He increased that to three and four words. Soon he could read six and eight words in a single eye span. After that, it wasn't long before he could read an entire line at one glance. Not satisfied with that, he practiced reading two lines at a time. Remember, that is with one single eye movement. Then he began to "zigzag" his way down the page, reading a half a paragraph at one glance. Finally, he could see one paragraph with one eye movement. Just two or three eye jumps and the entire page was finished! He would quickly zip his eyes down the page in a zig zag fashion, then turn the page, reading to digest the author's thoughts on the next page. Thumbing through a book at one sitting wasn't unusual for FDR.

JOHN F. KENNEDY

John F. Kennedy became an extremely fast reader after he took a course in speed reading. It is reported that his reading speed was approximately 284 WPM before he studied speed reading, but he worked at it until he could reach a speed of about 1,200 WPM. His great range of speed allowed him much flexibility to vary the rate on material as he saw fit. He often liked to use rapid eye-span movements to pick up key words and important phrases. He also liked to read in large groups of thought units. However, the real strength in his reading repertoire was his ability to use varying rates of speed for the numerous types of reading materials that came across his desk.

SOME CONTEMPORARY TV PERSONALITIES

With the amount of TV viewing done today, most of the home viewers have become familiar with the cue-cards held by the TV crew so that TV stars don't forget their lines. Cue cards are also used to tell TV personalities things like "cut," or "Time for a commercial." Perhaps the TV celebrity whose cue-card reading can be followed most easily is Dean Martin. His fixations are distinct and his eye-span movements are small enough for the viewer to see. Dean Martin in his early days on TV liked to poke fun at his reading of cue cards. He would mutter or stumble over the words, regressing and saying the words two or three times. The audience loved it because they identified with a reading experience they all had had.

More recently, Jr. Samples on the "Hee-Haw" show joked his way into the hearts of many with a similar style of regressing and making long fixations on cue cards. Here too, the audience finds this reading process amusing because they identify with it. They either go through it themselves or have seen many other readers do so. We have all done these things at one time or another, and it is funny to see others do the same thing; but it is especially funny to see it on TV where usually we see the very best in sports and entertainment. We expect TV superstars to be super in everything they do, including reading, and when we see them make the same little human errors we all do, it makes us laugh and identify with them even more.

WALTER CRONKITE and HARRY REASONER

These TV newscasters are familiar to millions of Americans. Their eye movements are readily distinguishable as they read the news from the prepared reports before them. Their eye-span movements are excellent. They read in large groups of thought units and even talk in such a style. Listen to their next news reports and see for yourself. I have never seen them use any motor movements to read, (discussed in chapter 4) and they very seldom regress. Their reading rates appear to be far above average which is a factor that contributes to their success in reading the nightly news reports.

10

Obstacles to Overcome

You have now completed nine chapters of this book and through them you've become a better reader. You have improved your reading skills, habits, and attitudes. You are much more knowledgeable about reading and your own reading abilities. For example: (1) You've learned to determine what your reading needs are and how to meet them. (2) You've learned how your reading skills compare to others of comparable or similar educational background. (3) You've learned to read faster and faster. (4) You've learned to improve your comprehension. (5) You've learned to become a balanced reader, able to apply different reading skills to different reading situations.

You have actually measured many of your new reading gains. All the tests you've taken on the various paragraphs or readings show your reading speed and comprehension and actually demonstrate your progress. But no matter how great your reading progress has been, you can surely continue to make further gains. How to do this now becomes the question. You might ask, how have others done it? How have others continued to improve? Or maybe the question is, what has kept them from achieving the high reading speeds they desire? After almost twenty years of teaching speed reading, I've concluded there are eight major reasons why many people don't achieve the high reading skills they desire. They are briefly presented as follows:

1. *Small Eye Span.* Some people see single letters instead of whole words when they read. Their eye span is so small that they don't even read one word at a time. Obviously, their reading speed goes along at a snail's pace. In order to read faster, they must master the eye-span technique, for this is the primary determinant in controlling their reading rate or potential. Most people can read at least one word at a time, so for them to read faster is a matter of increasing the eye span from one word to two words at a single glance. From two words, their eye span can go to three or four or five, depending on motivation, amount of practice, etc. Some people are critical of reading like this and claim that such fast reading automatically means poor reading. This is not true. If the reading process is such that the reader is more efficient, finishes a selection faster and more easily, and comprehends more (or even the same amount) at a higher rate of speed, who is to say that is poor reading? In fact, it is generally true that the slow readers are less sure about the meaning of what they are reading than the fast readers. It is slower readers who generally have reading problems until they master these skills.

Research has shown distinctly (and beyond debate) exactly how the eyes move in reading. It is up to us to utilize these modern findings to improve our eye movements in the reading process. It is essential that you understand how and why the eyes move in the manner they do in order to read. That's what this book has been showing you. Your mind and your eyes can take in more than one word at a glance. Many people are held back only by their habit of a poor eye span. They have read one word at a time for so long it is difficult for them to change. That's where practice and patience come in. They can change. Anyone can change—if they want to. Motivation and desire, along with the steps presented in this book, are the keys to better and faster reading.

2. *Regressing*. Retracing or re-reading is a time-consuming factor that burns up WPM and almost slows the reader down to a halt. It's like trying to win the Indianapolis 500 on race day with the driving style of backing up every other lap. Ridiculous, right? How can speed be attained if the driver backs up in the race or the reader goes backward over the material? Speed is obviously forward motion or, rather, rapid forward movement. Any backward movements thus serve to impede or reduce that speed. Of all the speed reading techniques the easiest to master is *eliminating regressions*. Of all the time-consuming factors, regression is the most commonly reported by people in my classes. Of all the wasted eye movements, regression is the one that people can overcome most easily and see immediate improvement after doing so.

Perhaps the important question is whether you simply want to regress or whether you regress from habit. Many times people go back over material and re-read words because they feel more comfortable doing that. It gives them a sense of security and the impression that they are comprehending more. They psych themselves into believing that they re-read words because it is good for them. They claim that they sacrifice speed for comprehension. The truth is, many people regress simply because it is a habit. Poor eyesight may be a valid cause for regression. A poor vocabulary may be another. But these reasons are not applicable to most people. This is not to say all of us do not regress now and then. However, these regressions should be few and far between. Controlling regressions is critical if you are to become a speed reader.

3. *Subvocalizing.* Reliance upon hearing the words mentally causes many readers not to read as fast as they want to. They're slowed down by waiting to hear the words mentally. They subvocalize their way through a book. This reliance creates an artificial roadblock or barrier to a high, flexible reading rate. It is usually the result of the way the reader was taught to read as a child and is the carry-over effect of still hearing the words even though this is no longer necessary. It is not uncommon to see students use this technique of vocalizing when they study or when they are confronted by a tough test. When the chips are down, many people "kick in" the extra senses (such as hearing by vocalizing) in order to get through the difficult material. That doesn't mean, however, that comprehension is any better because one hears the words or doesn't hear them for that matter. The question is really, what does relying on hearing words do to speed? And the obvious answer is that it slows it down.

4. *Reading Everything at the Same Speed.* This is probably the most commonly misunderstood aspect of reading I have ever seen. Most people were taught to read at one steady rate, and they subsequently apply this rate to all reading with few exceptions. They read novels at the same rate they read newspapers. Or they read the newspaper at the same rate they read their insurance policy. They blame the schools or their teachers and say, "No one ever taught me any differently." The truth is, in almost every elementary school I've seen, the emphasis is on teaching the child to read and not on rates of speed. Once the child is taught the mechanics of the reading process in first and second grade, the next three years are spent building vocabulary.

Very little or no effort is ever put into developing the child's reading rate. This may not be true in all schools, but I believe it to be the case in most.

People later on then take a speed reading course and their conceptual goal for the course is to be able to read *everything* at some remarkable new terrific rate. They, in essence, figure to cash in their old slow steady rate for one new high steady rate. This isn't what speed reading is all about. Let's compare the process to walking and running. Most people walk. Perhaps for some the goal is to walk faster or maybe run at a high rate of speed. They can learn to walk faster—how much faster depends on factors such as those we've explained in this book: practice, technique, motivation, physiological conditions, etc. But even those who get to be extremely fast runners can't maintain that rate for long. They usually wind up with varying rates based on a variety of factors. Such is the case in speed reading. The key is to vary the rate and not to read everything at one steady speed—fast or slow.

We might also compare reading to traveling in a car. If your goal is to go from Pittsburgh to Miami, varying conditions along the way demand varying speeds. No one would buy or want a car that goes only at one speed. Reading should be like driving—flexible, adaptable, and purposeful.

5. *Poor Concentration.* I often hear statements like this. "If I could only concentrate, I'd get good grades," or, "If I could concentrate, I could read faster, but I get tired easily. I guess my attention span is too short." A businessman once said to me, "I'd give a thousand dollars to learn to keep my mind on what I am reading. I'm often aware that I have not been paying attention. I think about a multitude of things when I read. I watch others around me. I look away from the book. Look back. Try to find my place again. Read a little bit more. Daydream for a while. Think about other things. Then read some more. Pretty soon I'm bored. I figure my concentration is bad. I see others who sit for hours and don't move and just read. I wish I could do that."

This kind of experience is common. It happens to everyone at one time or another. But you can learn to concentrate if you realize that poor concentration is one of your reading problems. The fallacy about concentration is that many people think it can be overcome by regressing or making long fixations or reading slowly. What these people fail to realize is that a moderate or fast rate of speed forces us to pay attention. It's when we read slowly that our minds have time to daydream and wander. If they're in a hurry to get somewhere and get a job done, most people don't fool around—they go right about accomplishing the task. It's the person who sees no time factor or no purpose in a task who is slow, dreamy, indifferent, and lacks the power of concentration. Fast readers are usually good readers. Slow readers are often poor readers. Not always, but often.

Speed and comprehension skills go together like bread and butter. They can't be isolated. As you raise your reading speed, you raise your ability to comprehend. You're actually comprehending faster—and usually in greater amounts because you are concentrating more. With greater reading speed, you cover more material, get more ideas, grasp more thoughts, gain a broader understanding, and retain more—all in the given amount of time. If you had that same amount of time and just browsed through the book, how would the results (speed and comprehension) compare?

6. *Reading Every Word Unnecessarily.* The reverence for the printed word is awesome. Many people don't dare to skip a word or phrase or sentence because they would feel guilty. Or they would feel they had missed something. This is truly a delusion. Every word printed or said is not of equal importance, and it is an unwise use of human talent and energy to apply them equally to every word. Tests have demonstrated that when we listen to another person speaking, we do not hear each and every word. We hear the words we need to hear. We in essence hear *a thought stream.* Well, in reading the same phenomenon is possible. You can train yourself to read by seeing merely the words you need to see. Moreover, when reading fast, you may find you are as close to the writer's stream of thought as if you were trying to read each word. Unimportant words get in the way and slow you down. Most authors never mean their readers to hang on every word in every sentence in every paragraph on every page. When you have finished this book will you remember all the words? Obviously not. Can you remember every word of every conversation you've had today? Obviously not. People have to learn the skill of applying *selective hearing* and selective listening and selective reading. That isn't to be confused with hearing only what you want to hear or reading into material only what you want to find. It is the process of accurately and quickly, with a minimum amount of effort, tuning into the message another person is trying to convey.

7. *Lack of Drive.* Some people are slow readers simply because they don't force themselves to read faster or break old habits. It's easier to just go along and settle for less. That's like Sally, who came to my classes and after the first lesson said, "You know what my problem is? I need to wear glasses. I have 'em at home, but I'm too lazy to wear 'em. They're a pain. I'm always losing them, anyhow."

I've purposefully avoided discussions in this book about poor vision or mental or emotional blocks to reading because I've made what I think are some very basic assumptions, about people . . . such as that if Sally took care of her poor vision, she could master the techniques shown in this book. I've assumed that if Joe would stop fighting his desire to improve his reading, he too could master the steps shown in this book. I've assumed that this book is for readers like you who have the will, the ability, and the determination to accept these concepts, apply them to their own reading styles, and emerge better, faster, and stronger readers.

There is no easy answer for lack of drive. The bottom line is and has to be—*it's up to you*. I can only *show you* how to speed read. You have to have the energy and the physiological and mental ability to make the eyes and brain work in the manner described in this book. The average person can do it.

8. *Overconcern with Comprehension.* Everybody wants to read at a zillion words per minute or some such fantastic rate they deem applicable to their self-concept. There's nothing wrong with that. The only problem is that many people want to learn to do this without any effect on their comprehension rate—up or down, good or bad, better or worse. You might take exception to the first statement, "Everybody wants to . . ." But let's look at America in general. We now live in a society where there is a great emphasis on speed: e.g., fast cars are better than slow cars, fast-food stores are extremely popular because they're fast, there's an *express checkout* in the grocery store for people in a hurry, fast typists are held in high esteem. Taking a short course, mastering a skill in a hurry, completing the job quickly, reading fast—the examples go on and on. The fact is, we now live in a society where there is a premium on speed.

This all brings us back to the point that learning to read fast can be done easily, but not without some effect on the rate of comprehension. That effect can be temporary or permanent, depending on the individual and a whole host of other variables. In teaching people to speed read, however, I have found that too many people spend so much time thinking about their comprehension that their energies for better reading skills are thwarted. Maybe it is a matter of priorities. In teaching speed reading, speed has to come first. Once speed is established, practice will bring comprehension and accuracy. It is a matter, let us say, of acclimation. Some people don't have what it takes to hang in there long enough. Their obvious immediate reaction is to drop the speed back again. That in turn restores the comprehension because the brain is used to functioning at that lower speed. So the cycle starts and repeats itself over and over again. Speed is not attained because comprehension lags. Comprehension is calling the shots. This is unfortunate, for all one needs to do is practice and bear with the new reading speed and, above all, vary the rate. Comprehension will soon be established as the mind adjusts to receiving data at a new faster rate. Once that is done, in fact, comprehension is usually better than ever, for as was said earlier, there is less time for irrelevant thought processes when the mind must deal with data coming in rapidly.

The eight factors just discussed have caused some people to fall short of their reading expectations. On the other hand more people have gone on to achieve the speed and comprehension they want. They are well satisfied with their newfound reading skills. There is no age restriction on success in reading. Records are made to be broken. With the aid of modern technology, reading has been refined to a skill anyone who is predisposed to can master. Remember, you don't have to regress! You can vary the rate and read faster than ever! You can zoom right through the material!

Try the next two exercises and record your time on the Progress Chart in the back of the book.

READING #21
TAX SAVINGS FOR ENERGY SAVERS

Homeowners and renters should take advantage of the tax savings made available by recent federal laws. These new laws include the National Energy Act, which establishes several tax incentives for encouraging energy conservation and installing alternative energy equipment. Under this new act, individuals are allowed substantial tax credit for money spent on the purchase and installation of energy conservation devices such as insulation, storm doors, windows, caulking, weather-stripping and certain automatic thermostats. The new tax credit also includes the installation of solar, geothermal, or wind-powered energy-producing equipment. Additional information on energy credits in the new tax code (Publication 903) is available from IRS offices throughout the country.

Mark the following statements either True (T), False (F), or Not Mentioned (N).

1. There is a recent tax law encouraging energy conservation.

———————

2. The new tax law on energy conservation was passed in 1979.

———————

3. Even storm windows and caulking are included under the tax incentive credits. _____

4. Publication 903 contains detailed information about the new tax law. _____

5. Tax credits are not extended to solar and geothermal energy sources. _____

Time/Sec.	2	3	4	5	6	7
WPM	3630	2420	1815	1452	1210	1037

If your time isn't shown, divide into 7260 the number of seconds it took you to read the paragraph. That'll give you your exact WPM. (For answers, see page 147.) Place your scores on the Progress Chart page in the back.

READING #22
WHY PEOPLE SAY THEY READ

Why do people read? The amount of reading done by modern Americans is of great interest to some people. In today's TV-watching society, how much do people actually read? In most research being reported today, studies are concluding that approximately 90 percent of the Americans sampled say they have read a book or magazine within the last six months. That statistic varies from study to study, but one conclusion is rather obvious—an overwhelming majority of Americans read something more complicated than street signs and advertisements on billboards. The most common reason given by most people for reading was "general knowledge," followed closely by pleasure or leisure-recreation reading. Either third or fourth on most lists was "to obtain knowledge for work, job or career." Thus, it is quite clear that most Americans (in spite of recent claims to the contrary) still spend a great deal of time reading; and their single most important reason for reading is to obtain general knowledge.

Mark the following statements either True (T), False (F), or Not Mentioned (N).

1. Most Americans no longer read much due to the amount of TV being watched. _____
2. Recent studies show a great majority of Americans do read. _____
3. The major reason cited by most people for reading is to obtain general knowledge rather than for leisure or relaxation. _____
4. Most people read to fulfill educational requirements. _____
5. The second most frequently cited reason for reading comes under the heading of leisure or relaxation. _____

Time/Sec.	2	3	4	5	6	7
WPM	5130	3420	2565	2052	1710	1466

If your time isn't shown, divide into 10,260 for your exact WPM. (For answers, see page 147.)

11

Reading Machines

Are there other options which haven't been discussed in this book but that you can try which will improve your reading speed and comprehension? Obviously, the answer is yes, for no one book can possibly describe every step that can be used to improve one's reading skills. The ones presented thus far have proven to be the most successful with most people I have taught. That was the criterion for including them in this book. They are the major keys to improving your reading style—whether it be for informational, educational, career, or recreation purposes.

Many reading centers at large universities have tried different kinds of training devices on reading machines to improve reading skills. Sometimes these machines have proven to be of immense value when used in conjunction with theories, steps, techniques, or concepts like those presented in this book. One such machine, called the *ophthalmograph,* actually photographs your eye movements as you read a page; then the lines on the film give you the number of fixations made on the material you have just read. The film thus shows the number of words you read with each eye span. Such knowledge, combined with a thorough understanding of what fixations and eye span are, and of what can be done to improve these areas, can serve to make a much better reader. However, using the machines without understanding the fixation concept would greatly reduce their effectiveness. You should be leery of total reliance on machines to improve your reading style.

Another reading machine, the *tachistoscope,* is like a camera shutter that opens and closes, allowing images (usually printed words or phrases) to be seen by the reader for fractions of a second. Thus the reader is forced to read with little hesitation. The eye span must be rapid. Fixations must be few and very short in duration. Subvocalizing is greatly reduced since one cannot say the words fast enough to keep up with the shutter as it opens and closes, flashing the series of words before the viewer's eyes. The idea is that what the reader learns on the screen in terms of eye movements can be transferred to the printed page.

The tachistoscope is actually a very old invention. Thousands of years ago the Greeks were concerned that they couldn't read their scrolls fast enough. They invented the tachistoscope, which in Greek means swift viewing. The Greeks' tachistoscope (or speedioscope) was very much like the reading-window card shown in chapter 2. The Greeks, of course, didn't have camera shutters, so they used the reading-window card to increase their recognition rate so that they could see more words at one time as they read down the scroll. Their method was lost for many years. Some say that it enjoyed a slight revival around 1900, but it wasn't until the technological revolution of the World War II period that the concept of a tachistoscope was dusted off and revitalized.

Many pilots are still trained to recognize other aircraft by a technique similar to the tachistoscope or speedioscope. This is a process in which silhouettes of aircraft are flashed for a fraction of a second on a screen, and the pilots must accurately identify so many aircraft. I have often had pilots, or former pilots, in speed reading classes; and it is amazing to see their average starting speed to be in the 300, 400, even 500 WPM range, largely because their eyes have been trained to move quickly and accurately by hours of tachistoscopic training. Their training in eye movements and quick recognition carried over into their reading.

Another interesting aspect of tachistoscopic training in recent years has been its newfound use by pro football teams. Some of them train quarterbacks to see and identify more players more rapidly. The opposing linebackers sometimes key their defense off the quarterback's eye movements. Eye fixation patterns made by quarterbacks are easily detected by linemen. A regression as the quarterback scrambles in the backfield looking for a receiver is sometimes even noticeable to the TV viewer, as the ballplayer's head turns or his eyes sweep back. Some pro quarterbacks have spent hours on tachistoscopes training their eyes to make fewer fixations and still see more rapidly and accurately. Eye patterns of baseball players are important as well.

A tachistoscope can be purchased quite inexpensively for individual home use. They sell for as low as $5 to $10 with perhaps as many as a thousand slides so that the viewer can flash the shutter and read many different words, numbers, or phrases. They can usually be purchased at any store carrying educational equipment. Most schools and universities have such machines readily available. Some public libraries also have this equipment available for readers to use at the library or to check out. There are slides made for all reading levels, from preschool to teenage to college to adult. In ordering a tachistoscope, one should specify the level of reading material to be included on the slides.

The tachistoscope has recently taken on a new name. It is now frequently being called an *eye-span trainer,* since that is its basic function. This machine trains the eyes to move in a certain span: two, three, four, five, six, eight words at a time. The material is shown for controlled periods of time as brief as one-hundredth of a second. The slowest speed is usually one second. It isn't difficult to learn to see two or three words at a single glance before the shutter closes on the eye-span trainer. If your major concern is to improve and increase your eye span, you may want to consider using the eye-span trainer *in conjunction* with the theories presented in this book.

Another reading device, now usually restricted to use by large reading centers or schools or universities, is the *reading film.* The reading student is shown a series of films and asked to read the words as they appear on the screen and to keep up with the rate at which the words are shown. Of course, each film grows progressively quicker as the words are shown faster and faster to the reader. After each film, the reader is asked to take a comprehension quiz. The films are designed to help readers improve their reading skills in the area of eye span, fixations, recognition rate, regressions, and vocalizing. These films are usually very expensive and are, of course, limited in the number of topics available. Depending upon one's reading interests, the films may or may not be appealing. Consideration of expense and practicality, however, all but prohibit the purchase of these films by the individual for home use.

A machine that has many variations, though they all perform the same function, is the *reading pacer,* sometimes called a reading accelerator. This machine and the eye-span trainer are the two most common, most popular, and most successful reading machines used today. A reading pacer or accelerator usually has a sloped platform on which you can place a book or magazine of your choice. Thus, you can read whatever material you like. You then set the pacer at the desired rate of so many words per minute. Most pacers have a range of 200–2,000 WPM. Pacers with a higher range, up to 10,000 WPM, are available but cost more. Some pacers I've seen even come with a red light that goes on when a person is reading above 4,000 WPM. For many readers that provides an incentive to hit a speed high enough to turn on the light. When I first saw a reading machine like that it reminded me of the bell people try to ring at a carnival or amusement park, using what looks like a big sledgehammer to hit a small platform which in turn sends up a metal weight to ring the bell at the top of a twelve- to fifteen-foot pole. I'm not knocking this technique; both the bell and the pacer have proved to be highly successful. One is an incentive to show physical strength, the other to show reading strength.

In any event, the reading pacer works like this: You place your reading material under the machine, set the desired WPM, and then a barlike piece of metal or beam of light descends over the page while you are reading. The descending bar of light prevents regressing or re-reading. It is designed to force you to read at the desired rate, or WPM. You may accelerate or slow it down as you wish, depending on your abilities, the purpose, type of material being read, etc. I have found this device especially good for reducing vocalizing or subvocalizing. It really pushes your recognition rate and can be ideal for forcing you to read in thought units or large groups of words. By setting the pacer faster and faster you may increase your reading rate as well as your ability to concentrate. It should be noted that both the eye-span trainer and pacer have been used to increase powers of concentration.

When I was in the Air Force, we were given a course in speed reading. The instructor set the WPM on the pacer up higher and higher each day. It was difficult at first to keep up. I thought my comprehension was practically zero. I could catch glimpses of the material, but I was missing so much as the bar descended down each page at an even faster clip that I became rather frustrated. Once I no longer relied on reading every word and eliminated my regression habit, I began to pick up speed and comprehension. Then the instructor set the machine back from 1,200 WPM to about 450 WPM. Suddenly, reading at 450 was a breeze, though it was something I couldn't do before I took that course. I had started at 200 WPM, so 450 with 80 percent comprehension seemed to me to be a remarkable accomplishment. What I did not know then was that after the course was over, I would gradually go back to my original speed. What was wrong? I later asked myself. The problem was I no longer had the machine to rely on and force me to read at 450 WPM. Without the periodic stimulation of the pacer, my reading speed dropped back. I took another course and began an intensive study on the subject of speed reading. This time the instructor explained what regressions were (along with other points, of course) and thus I began to see what the pacer had done for me: It eliminated my regressions temporarily, but without the proper understanding of what my eyes were doing and how the reading process worked, I had slipped back to my old reading rate and begun regressing again. The new awareness and understanding of regressions and their effect on reading immediately shot my speed upward to newer, greater speeds. I didn't need to rely on a reading machine. Once I knew what to do, for example, eliminate regressions, my efforts to improve my reading shifted from mechanical instruments and devices to book-centered practicing. The two together (reading machines and book-centered practice) can aid the reader to achieve new heights in reading speed. Based on my experience, however, I prefer the book-centered approach.

Research studies are not conclusive as to the relative merits of one type of training versus the other. Neither book- nor machine-centered practice will produce the very same results for everyone. Success depends upon so many factors within each individual's reading style and reading needs. I have found over the years that for most people, reading machines will provide initial stimulation to reach spectacular gains in a very short period of time. But the speed or new rate is not lasting and the individual's rate soon almost always declines—sometimes as rapidly as it went up. I have concluded that this is because the reader does not truly understand the reading process (e.g., regressions, eye span, etc.) and because he or she has not practiced long enough to change old reading habits into permanent new ones. What's more, since most reading is done without a machine, total reliance on mechanical devices is unrealistic. What usually happens when using such machines is that the reader reads like a demon for ten to fifteen minutes a day while on the machine, but then for the rest of the day reads in the regular way, complete with regressions and all the old slow habits.

Evidence clearly shows that book-centered practice, which is what this book is all about, is much more likely to result in steady and relatively permanent improvements in your reading speed and comprehension. There is no doubt that more and more reading centers, colleges, and universities are shifting to the book-centered approach. Even commercial schools, which once used a whole series of reading machines to attract the mechanically oriented American people, are now emphasizing the self-help approach as outlined in this book.

The acceleration and improvement of your reading is important. It is only through your own efforts that your reading will become better than ever. Because reading is a human process, the person who pushes a button on a machine and then sits back expecting that machine to improve his or her reading is bound to be disappointed. Even this book cannot do it for you. It takes individual effort to change your reading skills. Take small steps, work at them gradually, set definite goals, and follow a routine as shown by the examples in chapter 5. These are all part of the journey to better reading. You can't expect your reading to change by itself. Motivation and willpower combined with the tips and know-how explained in this book will unlock the powers of speed and comprehension for you. These techniques have worked for thousands of students I've taught over the years—from elementary-age students to senior citizens and Ph.D.'s. And yet, I must tell you the most powerful force to change your reading style is you—YOU, yourself.

Try the following two paragraphs and remember—go for SPEED . . . SPEED . . . SPEED.

READING #23
BICYCLING

One of the newest crazes to hit the modern American public is bicycling. From suburbia to the inner city, bicycle sales are booming. Bicycling seems to have an appeal to people of all ages. It has especially caught on with those who don't want to get into jogging but who still want to get their bodies in shape. Latest physiological research indicates runners and cyclists have much in common in the results obtained such as good physical fitness, lean and tightened muscles, an air of exhilaration, pride of accomplishment, and mental alertness. Those who enjoy bicycling say it is simple, inexpensive, easy, natural, and never boring. Those who excel in the art of cycling say the secret is pace—the steady, rhythmic movement of legs. They say it is acquired through practice and once mastered, enables one to consistently cycle farther, longer, and more easily . . . and feel better.

Mark the following statements either True (T), False (F), or Not Mentioned (N).

1. Bicycling is one of the latest crazes in America. _____
2. Aerobics is just as good for your physical fitness as cycling. _____
3. Bicycling is expensive. _____
4. Results of cycling are similar to running or jogging. _____
5. The secret to the art of cycling is in the steady pace. _____

Time/Sec.	2	3	4	5	6	7	8
WPM	4590	3060	2295	1836	1530	1311	1147

Divide into 9180 for your exact WPM if your time isn't shown. (For answers, see page 148.)

READING #24
SAVE THE TREES

We hear a lot about endangered animal species. Well, quite possibly the world's forest lands could also be in danger of extinction. For all the years people have inhabited the earth, trees have been a source of fuel, building material, profit and inspiration. Legends tell of Buddha and Joan of Arc meditating beneath trees; the Druids of ancient Britain worshipped trees, and trees even figure largely in the early tales of the Hindus and Hebrews. Now forests are threatened as never before in earth's history. Man himself is lessening his quality of life, for large wooded areas are vital to the quality of soil, air, and water. Man is simply cutting down the world's forests at an alarmingly accelerating rate. What is needed to offset this potential disaster is reforestation and proper management of today's resources. The delicate balance of nature and the ecological cycle is vitally important to the quality of human life for us as well as future generations to come. Thus, "saving the trees" can be an important contribution from this generation to those that follow.

Mark the following statements either True (T), False (F), or Not Mentioned (N).

1. Trees in some parts of the world might be considered endangered species. _____

2. Trees have been a source of fuel, building material and inspiration. _____

3. Trees play a vital role in the quality of air, soil and water.

   _____

4. The quality of human life is dependent on the balance of nature. _____

5. What is needed to offset the devastation of forests is reforestation and management of resources. _____

Time/Sec.	2	3	4	5	6	7
WPM	5550	3700	2775	2220	1850	1585

If your time isn't shown, divide into 11,100 for your WPM. (See page 148 for answers.)

12

Practice Exercises

The following exercises are provided to give you additional opportunities to continue mastering your newfound reading skills. The Progress Chart in the back has been designed so that you can continue to keep a record of your development. In any program of self-improvement systematic practice over an extended period of time is most effective.

Time works on your side. Try to keep a certain amount of time set aside each day for practice. Apply yourself wholeheartedly and watch your progress. See and feel your success! After practicing, try several of these readings and quizzes each day. (See pages 148–150 for answers.)

Watch your progress continue. From time to time you may want to refer back to this book for a few refreshing tips and even re-read some of these practice exercises just to see how you are doing. For comparison purposes, you may find that rather interesting. You'll be amazed how you have corrected your old reading weaknesses and learned new reading skills!

READING #25
THE TACHISTOSCOPE HELPS IMPROVE YOUR READING

One fundamental value of tachistoscopic training is that it teaches students how to see quickly and accurately whatever material is shown to them. It also helps to widen the span of vision so that the student is able to see more words at each glance. It has been proven that when a reader learns to see accurately as many as twice the number of words or numbers he could see before beginning the tachistoscopic training, reading speed will correspondingly increase. Other factors like fatigue, which sometimes results from prolonged reading, are usually reduced or may even be eliminated by such training. The tachistoscope helps improve your reading.

In this and all the following reading exercises mark each statement either True (T), False (F), or Not Mentioned (N).

1. Tachistoscopic training increases reading speed. _____

2. Fatigue from long periods of reading may be eliminated. _____

3. Tachistoscopic training reduces the number of words or numbers read at a single glance. _____
4. Such training helps the reader to learn to concentrate. _____
5. Most speed reading schools have tachistoscopes for teaching speed reading. _____

Time/Sec.	1	2	3	4	5	6
WPM	6960	3480	2320	1740	1392	1160

If your time in seconds is not shown above, divide into 6960 for your WPM.

READING #26
BETTER READING=MORE INCOME

A better job with higher pay may actually result from one's ability to read and obtain more education. In this age of speed, the person who can do more work in less time usually is rewarded by increased income or more leisure time. Most of us are interested in such benefits, and thus the number of people who spend time and money to improve their reading is increasing daily. Since most of us can double or triple our reading efficiency, the gains we might derive from such self-improvement can be great indeed. You might then say that better reading equals more income.

1. The number of people spending time and money to improve their reading is decreasing every day. _____
2. Most of us can double or triple our reading efficiency. _____
3. More leisure time can result from better reading. _____
4. Schools should teach these speed reading techniques. _____
5. Better reading equals more income. _____

Time/Sec.	1	2	3	4	5
WPM	6660	3330	2220	1665	1332

If your time isn't shown, divide into 6660. Don't forget to keep track of your continued improvement by using the Progress Chart in the back of this book. You might find it interesting at this point to compare your reading speed and comprehension scores from, let's say, Reading #24 or #25 to Reading #1. The results will clearly show you how much progress you've made and how much better and faster you can now read as a result of using the tips and techniques found in this book.

READING #27
MAN IN MOTION

Because of the great success the pro football teams like the Dallas Cowboys have had using the "man-in-motion" principle, it would behoove coaches to seriously consider including it in their offensive strategies. One reason the "motion offense" has been so successful is that it forces the defense to cover the entire width of the field. Thus, by allowing the man in motion to gain greater lateral movement, the defensive secondary is forced to cover the width of the field. Also by allowing the motion man to move beyond the wide receiver to the side he is moving, the motion man can be used to take the double coverage off a wide receiver. This allows greater strength to a team with a volatile quarterback with a good passing arm and a wide receiver with a good pair of hands. More and more coaches are beginning to look at the man-in-motion principle and how they can work it into their offense.

1. "Man in motion" is a football offensive strategy. _____
2. The Dallas Cowboys have had much success with this play. _____
3. The New York Jets and the Miami Dolphins use a similar offense. _____
4. The man in motion restricts lateral movement. _____
5. The defensive secondary is forced to cover the entire width of the field against the man in motion. _____

Time/Sec.	2	3	4	5	6
WPM	5070	3380	2535	2028	1690

If your time in seconds is not shown divide into 10,140 for your WPM.

READING #28
DARE TO LOVE

She sighed . . . and then felt her heart leap as the double doors suddenly swept open again. Their dark panels framed one of the tallest men she had ever seen, lithe and erect, wearing knee boots of gleaming leather moulded to the strong calves of his legs. Blue denims were belted into a flat, athletic waist and a fine white T-shirt covered a broad chest and a pair of wide shoulders. The neck of his T-shirt was open against a suntanned throat, and as her gaze rose to his face . . . she knew instantly why she had been fascinated by and dared to love this man. Stories like this are more fun to read if you can speed read!

1. He wore tan breeches. _____
2. She was a tall, statuesque blonde. _____
3. He was one of the tallest men she had ever seen. _____
4. She knew instantly why she dared to love him. _____
5. He had on an open blazer. _____

Time/Sec.	1	2	3	4	5
WPM	7440	3720	2480	1860	1488

Divide into 7440 for your WPM if your time isn't shown.

READING #29
ANIMALS

Beware of traps! The trapping of animals is not something that always happens in far-off places like Alaska, Hudson Bay or Siberia. It can take place close to your home. Illegal trapping may be going on near a stream or wooded area near you. This trapping may be for "furs for profit" from raccoons, foxes or other game animals. There is no doubt that trapping is cruel—no matter where it takes place, but if it is going on in your neighborhood it can threaten the well-being of your pet dog or cat or even an unsuspecting child. For your own safety and that of your children and pets, you should keep animals leashed and caution children if they play in the woods or fields where traps may be set. If you find an illegal trap, report it to your local humane society and to the state fish and game authorities.

1. Traps are only found in places like Alaska, Hudson Bay or Siberia. _____
2. Trapping is cruel no matter where it takes place. _____
3. The most valuable animal trapped is the beaver. _____
4. If you find an illegal trap you should report it to the authorities. _____
5. Trapping never takes place near residential areas. _____

Time/Sec.	1	2	3	4	5
WPM	9360	4680	3120	2340	1872

Divide into 9360 if your time isn't shown above.

READING #30
THE DESIRE TO EXCEL

The human race has long had a passion to excel in everything it does. People all over the world continually demonstrate the courage to accomplish things they'd never even dared to attempt before. Exhilarating people, great ideas, remarkable skills, and performances of cherished excellence in all fields are respected by the world's people everywhere. The free human spirit, the zest for new beginnings, and the challenge of new horizons to conquer, the courage to take risks and try one's best—even if the net result is failure—truly marks the greatness in the human race and the liveliest people among us. What constantly astonishes people is that the desire to excel is always there among all of us. Turn loose your potential and you may discover more about yourself and your own inner strength than you've ever known before.

1. The desire to excel is universal. _____
2. Performances of excellence are respected by people everywhere. _____
3. You have great potential if you turn it loose. _____
4. People don't have to fail. _____
5. Most people don't have great unused potential inside themselves. _____

Time/Sec.	1	2	3	4	5	6
WPM	8940	4470	2980	2235	1788	1490

Divide into 8940 for your WPM if your time isn't shown.

READING #31
THE NEW COMPUTER TOY

The home computer is coming! Already on the market and in many homes, the home computer is either a magnificent toy or the first step toward something more complex to come. What you get out of this new-fangled home computer depends on how much money and effort you put in. It will entertain you or stretch your mind, but don't think it will simplify your life. One computer comes with prepackaged programs to let you play TV games and figure household finances by filling in the blanks. You're not required to do any programming because you use their system to organize and store your records and calculate results. Then there's the home computer that comes with a few games, but you learn programming with their manual. (That's a little like learning a foreign language.) Once you learn the computer language or programming techniques you can create new tasks for the machine to do. You can find these new home computers in electronic or computer stores across the country.

1. Home computers are coming. _____
2. The computer can be used as a toy to play TV games. _____
3. IBM invented the first home computer. _____
4. Learning to program a computer is like learning a foreign language. _____
5. You can't create new tasks for any of the computers, as they are already programmed. _____

Time/Sec.	1	2	3	4	5	6
WPM	10,560	5280	3520	2640	2112	1760

Divide into 10,560 for your WPM if you need to.

READING #32
THE MG . . . BRITAIN'S GREAT LITTLE SPORTS CAR

Britain has a great classic sports car known as the MG. People who own these cars tell me it is great fun to put the top down and feel the sun on your face, the wind in your hair and all the vibrant action that comes with a ride in a fast sports car. These classic sports cars are born of a new lifestyle of competition and speed. They offer a four-speed stick shift, precision rack and pinion steering, a stout-hearted motor offered in varying dimensions, front disc brakes—and remarkable agility, stamina and handling. They are said to be a whole lot of fun to drive. So drive one soon and see for yourself what a great sports car Britain has in its classic little MG.

1. Britain's great classic sports car is the Jaguar. _____
2. People say riding in a sports car is fun. _____
3. The British sports car mentioned in the paragraph comes with rack and pinion steering. _____
4. The sports car was not born out of competition and speed.

   _____
5. The Porsche is Europe's fastest racing sports car. _____

Time/Sec.	1	2	3	4	5	6
WPM	8040	4020	2680	2010	1608	1340

Divide into 8040 for your WPM if your time isn't shown.

READING #33
TODAY'S TEEN-AGERS SAY SCHOOLS AREN'T HARD ENOUGH

About half of America's teen-agers rate their schools an *A* or *B* for excellent or good marks, but say they don't have to work hard enough. Results of a recent Gallup Youth Poll for the Kettering Foundation show that approximately 50 percent of the 13- to 18-year-olds say they aren't asked by their schools to work hard enough in their studies. It is also interesting to note that four in ten youngsters say they enjoy school "very much." Other findings in Gallup's Youth Poll show that 79 percent feel America is still the land of opportunity and 88 percent of the teen-agers are willing to perform community services in exchange for high-school credit.

1. Teen-agers say schools today aren't hard enough on them.
   _____

2. Most students today say they like school. _____

3. Students no longer see America as a land of opportunity.
   _____

4. About 88 percent of today's teen-agers are willing to perform community service for high-school credit. _____

5. These findings are based on a Gallup poll. _____

Time/Sec.	1	2	3	4	5	6
WPM	7560	3780	2520	1890	1512	1260

Divide into 7560 for your WPM if your time isn't shown.

READING #34
AUTOMATIC PROTECTION SYSTEMS IN CARS OF THE FUTURE

By 1984 it is said that all new American cars will come equipped with either air bags or automatic seat belts. How well they succeed depends on several factors—including public acceptance. Car buyers in the future will have a choice between two automatic protection systems for passengers—the air bag or the automatic seat belt. Both are intended to protect front-seat occupants from serious or fatal injury in frontal or front-angle crashes up to 30 mph. It is estimated that such protection would save 9,000 lives and prevent more than 100,000 serious injuries each year. New federal regulations require that such automatic protection equipment be installed in all new cars as standard equipment beginning in 1984. Such protection is needed in automobile accidents because it is the "second crash" (the slamming of occupants against interior surfaces) that is so deadly, not the initial crash of the auto smashing against something in its path. The cars of the future will certainly be safer for all occupants.

1. By 1984 all American cars will come with air bags or automatic seat belts. _____
2. These are intended to protect the passengers from injury.
   _____
3. By 1984 all American cars will get better gas mileage. _____
4. Passengers will be protected from serious injury in frontal crashes up to 30 mph. _____
5. It is the initial impact of the crash that is so injurious to the passengers. _____

Time/Sec.	1	2	3	4	5	6
WPM	10,860	5430	3620	2715	2172	1810

Divide into 10,860 for your WPM if your time isn't shown.

READING #35
THE SUN SEEKERS

For many North Americans, the winter months of January, February and March are a time to seek the Florida sun. In mass exodus, the frozen northerners head south to places like Mexico or the islands, but most of all to Florida, where they spend about $1 billion each year. They find a sun-drenched land of wet T-shirt contests, relaxed sexuality, suntans, gentle surf, white sands, and reasonable prices. Canvas beach chairs, suntan lotion, sights to see, burnt arms, sunglasses, fun, and beautiful balmy weather are all a part of the scene that attracts people by the thousands to the sunny state of Florida each winter. "Going south" has become a ritual for many Americans who long to see the sunshine every winter.

1. For a few Americans, the month of March is a time to seek the Florida sun. _____
2. About $1 billion is spent in each year by the tourists. _____
3. The most popular Florida resort area is Ft. Lauderdale. _____
4. The most popular Florida resort area is Daytona Beach. _____
5. Suntan lotion, tans, gentle surf, white sands and balmy weather are part of the Florida scene. _____

Time/Sec.	1	2	3	4	5	6
WPM	7920	3960	2640	1980	1584	1320

Divide into 7920 for your WPM if your time isn't shown.

READING #36
ENJOY READING

There can be great enjoyment in picking up a good book for a few hours or an interesting magazine for a few moments of pleasure—if one knows how to read properly. However, if one finds reading a burdensome task which brings on headaches, watery eyes and sleepiness, then little enjoyment can be derived from such an experience. Since reading plays a necessary part in nearly all our lives, it behooves us to be rapid and comprehending readers. If one has developed improper reading habits, it is necessary to replace them with proper ones to achieve more benefits from our everyday reading. Books such as this help people improve their reading skills in speed and comprehension.

1. You can enjoy reading. _____
2. Reading plays a necessary part in all our lives. _____

3. Speed readers have more fun. _____
4. You can't replace improper habits with proper ones. _____
5. Books such as this help people improve their reading skills.

_____

Time/Sec.	1	2	3	4	5	6
WPM	7260	3630	2420	1815	1452	1210

Divide into 7260 for your WPM if your time isn't shown.

READING #37
MAKING A GOOD FIRST IMPRESSION

How people regard you intially can mean warm or cold feelings later on, for first impressions are often lasting impressions. First encounters or initial impressions are key factors that can determine success or failure in those critical moments such as job interviews, sales presentations, business luncheons or meeting his/her parents for the first time. There are some rules, which if followed, will help you create a positive image for yourself during those initial encounters. The first and most obvious impression is created by the way you dress. You should dress the way you want to be perceived. Second: Do your homework before you meet new people. Know a little about them. They'll be flattered you took the time, and it'll give you a basis for conversation. Next: Don't be late. Show that you respect their time. It's as valuable as yours. Fourth: Get the name and periodically use it in the conversation. Fifth and last: Listen. Don't dominate the conversation, and don't be the silent non-participant either. A good listener is still involved in the conversation. If you follow these rules, you'll make the first impression a good one!

1. First impressions are often lasting impressions. _____
2. Good talkers are good listeners. _____
3. The way you dress creates first impressions. _____
4. First encounters are key factors that can determine success or failure. _____
5. Being polite and courteous is another factor involved in first impressions. _____

Time/Sec.	1	2	3	4	5	6	7
WPM	12,300	6150	4100	3075	2460	2050	1757

Divide into 12,300 for your WPM if your time isn't shown.

READING #38
YOU CAN HAVE HEALTHIER, PRETTIER TEETH

Preventing tooth decay through proper care of teeth and gums is necessary if you want to have a pretty smile with pearly white teeth to smite that certain member of the opposite sex. Good nutrition is essential for the maintenance of firm, healthy tooth surfaces that resist tooth decay. Snacking on sweets and refined carbohydrates between meals or failing to clean teeth after snacks and after meals allows bacteria in the mouth to convert sugars and starches to powerful acids. These acids literally dissolve the calcium in the teeth to form holes where bacteria can live and multiply. Thus, you should avoid the use of sugar-sweetened foods and refined carbohydrates, brush after meals or at least rinse your mouth with water, and eat a balanced, nutritious diet. And it's absolutely imperative that you clean your teeth before retiring for the night. So turn your mousiest grin into a sparkling sunburst by following these smile-enhancing rules.

1. Good nutrition is essential for the maintenance of firm, healthy tooth surfaces. _____
2. Dental plaque is a soft, sticky substance that clings to your teeth, usually near the gum line. _____
3. You should brush after meals and before going to bed each night. _____
4. Snacking on refined carbohydrates isn't a factor in tooth decay. _____
5. Dental floss is an important aid to maintaining good healthy teeth. _____

Time/Sec.	1	2	3	4	5	6
WPM	9900	4950	3300	2475	1980	1650

Divide into 9900 for your **WPM** if your time isn't shown.

READING #39
A DIAMOND IS FOREVER

It starts with a diamond . . . and a promise to share their lives together . . . forever. That's when forever doesn't seem long enough for two people who are in love and want to spend the rest of their lives together. They promise to always be sensitive to each other's needs. And even after they're married, to always be there . . . sometimes just to listen. They promise to always be honest with each other and bring things out in the open where they can talk them over. They promise to share . . . and that's the part of their love they don't ever want to lose. A diamond is their promise to each other that they never will.

1. A diamond is forever. _____

2. A diamond is a promise they will always share and love each other. _____

3. Diamonds hold their value, and therefore are good investments. _____

4. Sometimes people want someone there just to listen. _____

5. For two people in love, forever doesn't seem long enough. _____

Time/Sec.	1	2	3	4	5	6
WPM	7140	3570	2380	1785	1428	1190

Divide into 7140 for your WPM if your time isn't shown.

FINAL READING CHECKLIST

* GOOD EYE SPAN!

* NO REGRESSIONS!

* VARY THE RATE!

* NO VOCALIZING!

* GOOD RECOGNITION RATE!

* REDUCE FIXATIONS!

* READ WITH A PURPOSE!

* KEEP AT IT!

Appendix A
Progress Chart

	SECONDS	WPM	COMPREHENSION
Reading # 1	24	295	40 PTS
Reading # 2	19	363	60 PTS.
Reading # 3	21	348	60 PTS.
Reading # 4	15	472	40 PTS
Reading # 5	20	390	80 PTS
Reading # 6			
Reading # 7			
Reading # 8			
Reading # 9			
Reading # 10			
Reading # 11			
Reading # 12			
Reading # 13			
Reading # 14			
Reading # 15			
Reading # 16			
Reading # 17			
Reading # 18			
Reading # 19			
Reading # 20			
Reading # 21			

	SECONDS	WPM	COMPREHENSION
Reading # 22	_____	_____	_____
Reading # 23	_____	_____	_____
Reading # 24	_____	_____	_____
Reading # 25	_____	_____	_____
Reading # 26	_____	_____	_____
Reading # 27	_____	_____	_____
Reading # 28	_____	_____	_____
Reading # 29	_____	_____	_____
Reading # 30	_____	_____	_____
Reading # 31	_____	_____	_____
Reading # 32	_____	_____	_____
Reading # 33	_____	_____	_____
Reading # 34	_____	_____	_____
Reading # 35	_____	_____	_____
Reading # 36	_____	_____	_____
Reading # 37	_____	_____	_____
Reading # 38	_____	_____	_____
Reading # 39	_____	_____	_____

Appendix B
Answers to Reading Exercises

Exercise # 1

1. T
2. N
3. N
4. N
5. F

Exercise # 2

1. F
2. N
3. N
4. T
5. T

Exercise # 3

1. F
2. N
3. T
4. F
5. T

Exercise # 4

1. F
2. T
3. F
4. N
5. T

Exercise # 5

1. T
2. N
3. F
4. N
5. T

Exercise # 6

1. F
2. N
3. T
4. T
5. T

Exercise #7

1. T
2. N
3. T
4. F
5. N

Exercise #8

1. T
2. N
3. F
4. T
5. T

Exercise #9

1. F
2. T
3. F
4. N
5. T

Exercise #10

1. T
2. T
3. N
4. F
5. T

Exercise #11

1. N
2. T
3. T
4. N
5. T

Exercise #12

1. T
2. T
3. T
4. T
5. T

Exercise #13

1. T
2. N
3. T
4. F
5. F

Exercise #14

1. F
2. T
3. N
4. T
5. F

Exercise # 15

1. F
2. F
3. T
4. N
5. N

Exercise # 16

1. T
2. T
3. T
4. F
5. N

Exercise # 17

1. T
2. N
3. T
4. N
5. T

Exercise # 18

1. T
2. N
3. T
4. T
5. T

Exercise # 19

1. T
2. N
3. F
4. T
5. N

Exercise # 20

1. N
2. N
3. T
4. T
5. F

Exercise # 21

1. T
2. N
3. T
4. T
5. F

Exercise # 22

1. F
2. T
3. T
4. N
5. F

Exercise # 23

1. T
2. N
3. F
4. T
5. T

Exercise # 24

1. T
2. T
3. T
4. T
5. T

Exercise # 25

1. T
2. T
3. F
4. N
5. N

Exercise # 26

1. F
2. T
3. T
4. N
5. T

Exercise # 27

1. T
2. T
3. N
4. F
5. T

Exercise # 28

1. F
2. N
3. T
4. T
5. F

Exercise # 29

1. F
2. T
3. N
4. T
5. N

Exercise # 30

1. T
2. T
3. T
4. N
5. F

Exercise #31

1. T
2. T
3. N
4. T
5. F

Exercise #32

1. F
2. T
3. T
4. F
5. N

Exercise #33

1. T
2. T
3. F
4. T
5. T

Exercise #34

1. T
2. T
3. N
4. T
5. F

Exercise #35

1. F
2. T
3. N
4. N
5. T

Exercise #36

1. T
2. T
3. N
4. F
5. T

Exercise #37

1. T
2. N
3. T
4. T
5. N

Exercise #38

1. T
2. N
3. T
4. F
5. N

150   APPENDIX B

Exercise #39

1. T
2. T
3. N
4. T
5. T

Index